Owls by Day and Night

Owls by Day and Night

Hamilton A. Tyler   Don Phillips

Naturegraph

Library of Congress Cataloging in Publication Data

Tyler, Hamilton A
  Owls by day and night.

  Bibliography: p.
  Includes index.
  1. Owls. 2. Birds—North America. I. Phillips,
Don, 1940-   joint author. II. Title.
QL696.S83T94   598.9'7'097   78-778

ISBN 0-87961-065-4 Cloth Edition
ISBN 0-87961-064-6 Paper Edition

Naturegraph Publishers, Inc., Happy Camp, California 96039

To all students and friends of owls—
and to the preservation of owl groves!

ACKNOWLEDGMENTS

When Don Phillips and I began this combined owl study, he agreed to draw the illustrations and also to report on those rare northern and eastern species which he has observed in the process of painting. His observations on these owls are now within the written text as well as on the plates. Don would like to thank the following easterners for information, photographs, and aid in locating owl subjects: Skip Boyer; Prof. Richard Clark, York College; Helen Krause, Anne Kutz; Jeffry Lapore; Thomas Wampler, Asst. Biologist, State of Penn.; Eugene Wingert, Appalachian Audubon Society; and Richard Zerbe. He would especially like to acknowledge the help of his wife, Esther Phillips, a fine nature photographer, who traveled with him on owl excursions from Canada to southern Mexico.

I would like to thank the following westerners for readings and criticisms of the manuscript at various stages and for their useful suggestions: Dr. John R. Arnold, Rod and Brenda Buchignani, Isabel Pember, Lynn Stafford, my wife Mary Tyler, and Clarence Wolcott. Joe T. Marshall, Jr., who is international in his owl interests and studies, read a version of this account and offered a number of corrections and explanations which have been used to advantage. I would like to thank the following for generously answering specific questions and for providing information on certain owls, or their eggs: Prof. Gordon D. Alcorn, University of Puget Sound; Larry A. Forbis, Wildlife Biologist, U. S. Forest Service; Gordon I. Gould, Jr., Assistant Wildlife Manager-Biologist, California Department of Fish and Game; Ed N. Harrison and Lloyd F. Kiff, Curator, Western Foundation of Vertebrate Zoology; Robert R. Maben, Staff Biologist, Oregon Department of Fish and Wildlife; Robert W. Nero, Manitoba Department of Renewable Resources, Wildlife Programs; and Jon Winter, Santa Rosa Junior College. I would also like to thank Robert R. Taylor for use of the superb flight photo of the Great Gray Owl. None of the helpful people named here are in any way responsible for errors which may occur in the final text. Lastly, I would like to thank the Editor, Sevrin Housen, not only for his diligence in matters of style and fact, but also for his enthusiasm about the subject, which is worthy of a true owlsman.

Hamilton A. Tyler
8450 West Dry Creek Road
Healdsburg, California 95448

CONTENTS

LIST OF TABLES

COMPLETE LIST OF ILLUSTRATIONS

INTRODUCTION

Each of the eighteen species of owls found within the boundaries of the United States and Canada has a personality of its own. The purpose of this book is to encourage readers to learn the differences and to begin thinking about each owl species as a separate "character." I have discussed "owlness," or those qualities common to all owls, in the following introductory section to provide background against which readers may judge the distinctive qualities exhibited by each owl. Once the bird watcher begins to think about the distinct kinds, rather than just "owls," their separate ways will become the focus of observation, and what before was just an abstract voice in the night or a droll figure perching by day will then be recognized as a fascinating subject for study. Furthermore, not many kinds of owls have been the object of detailed behavior studies; therefore, much that even a nonprofessional can learn through patient observation will not be found in books.

One of the important factors behind differences in owl personalities derives from extreme variations in size. If one thinks of all the kinds of sparrows it is very easy to draw them up together, in the mind, as being of "sparrow size;" there are larger sparrows and smaller ones of course, but all of these relate to our single vision of one size. Owls are quite different in this respect, since they range all the way from tiny creatures which may weigh two ounces or less, to majestic owls of several pounds which are borne aloft by a four- or five-foot wingspread. Size alone does not determine the personality entirely; the Pygmy Owl can be just as fierce as the Great Horned Owl, but the activity of a tiny, feisty owl is quite different from that of the lordly master who rules the woods. For that reason, I have commenced with a table giving weights, wingspread, and body size (see table 1, p. 14); the owls are listed in the sequence which follows so that the reader may become accustomed to this accepted scientific arrangement.

TABLE 1

Owl Sizes and Weights*

Name	Length**	Wingspread	Weight
Barn Owl	14"--20"	40"--47"	11--21 ozs.
Screech Owl	7"--10"	18"--24"	4--8 ozs.
Whiskered Owl	6.5"--8"	16"--20"	2.5--4.5 ozs.
Flammulated Owl	6"--7"	14"--19"	1.5--2.5 ozs.
Great Horned Owl	18"--25"	35"--55"	3--5 lbs.
Snowy Owl	20"--28"	54"--67"	3--6 lbs.
Hawk Owl	14"--17"	31"--35"	9--14 ozs.
Pygmy Owl	6"--7.5"	14.5"--16"	2--3ozs.
Ferruginous Owl	6"--7"	14.5"--16"	2--3 ozs.
Elf Owl	5"--6"	14"--15"	1-1.7 ozs.
Burrowing Owl	8.5"--11"	22"--24"	4.5--8 ozs.
Barred Owl	16"--24"	38"--50"	1--2.3 lbs.
Spotted Owl	16"--19"	42"--45"	1.1--1.7 lbs.
Great Gray Owl	24"--33"	48"--60"	1.7--3.3 lbs.
Long-eared Owl	13"--16"	36"--43"	6.5--12 ozs.
Short-eared Owl	13"--17"	38"--44"	7--17 ozs.
Boreal Owl	8"--12"	19"--25"	3--6 ozs.
Saw-whet Owl	7"--8.5"	17"--21"	2--4 ozs.

* One factor in the large spread in size and weight within a single species is that female owls (Burrowing Owl excepted) are larger than their respective males. Most other birds, except the diurnal birds of prey, show the opposite of this pattern, in that the males are larger. For simplicity the weights given above are roughly equivalent to those given in grams by (Earhart & Johnson, 1970). To convert to the metric system multiply: ounces X 28.3 for grams (or 28.349 for precision); inches X 25.4 for millimeters.

** Length refers to entire bird, from head to tail-tip.

RELATIVE SIZES OF LARGE OWLS   (Reduced scale)   **A** Great Horned Owl;
B Snowy Owl;   **C** Great Gray Owl;   **D** Barred Owl;   **E** Spotted Owl;   **F** Long-eared
Owl;   **G** Barn Owl;   **H** Short-eared Owl;   **I** Hawk Owl

RELATIVE SIZES OF SMALL OWLS   The scale of the owls in this illustration is 2½ times the scale on previous page. **A** Burrowing Owl; **B** Screech Owl; **C** Boreal Owl; **D** Saw-whet Owl; **E** Whiskered Owl; **F** Flammulated Owl; **G** Ferruginous Owl; **H** Pygmy Owl; **I** Elf Owl

Don Phillips 1976

PART I

GENERAL CHARACTERISTICS OF OWLS

UNDERSIDE WING PATTERNS: **A** Saw-whet Owl; **B** Barred Owl; **C** Great
Horned Owl; **D** Barn Owl

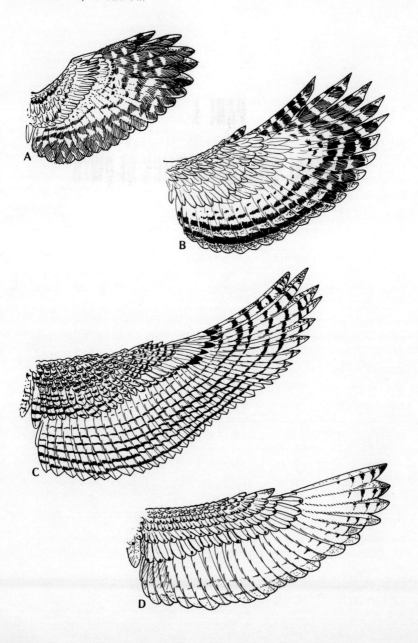

CHAPTER 1

HOW TO SEPARATE AND IDENTIFY OWLS

For the novice there may be a mild panic when first facing an unknown variety of owl—"it could be that species, but maybe it isn't; perhaps it is either . . ." and so on. After several species have come to mind there is likely to be more confusion than light shed by the available choices. To avoid, or at least reduce, this difficulty the species can be placed in several categories which are more easily held in the mind or readily referred to. These units will then allow one to discard the impossible choices and to consider only the species which might actually be the owl in question. There are eighteen species in the U. S. and Canada, and if these are separated into units based on distribution, size, color of the eyes, and the presence or absence of visible "ear" tufts or horns, then the choice will always be much smaller. First, let us consider distribution (see table 2 and the range maps which follow).

TABLE 2

Distribution of Owls in the U. S. and Canada

Owls Mainly Northern		
Snowy Owl	See range map 6	(strays south some winters)
Hawk Owl	See range map 7	
Great Gray Owl	See range map 14	(also in high mts. of the West)
Boreal Owl	See range map 17	

TABLE 2 – *Continued*

Owls Mainly Western		
Whiskered Owl	S. Ariz. & N.M.	See range map 3
Flammulated Owl	Mts. of West	See range map 4
Pygmy Owl	Mts. of West, incl. coast	See range map 8
Ferruginous Owl	S. Ariz. & S. Texas	See range map 9
Elf Owl	S.W. border	See range map 10
Burrowing Owl	All of West, plus	
	Central & S. Florida	See range map 11
Spotted Owl	N.W. Coast through Calif.	
	Cent. Rockies to W.	
	Texas & Arizona	See range map 13

Owl Basically Eastern		
Barred Owl	East of Rockies (except	
	scattered records to	
	coast in Wash. State	
	and British Columbia)	See range map 11

Owls Inhabiting Nearly the Entire Continent	
Great Horned Owl	See range map 5
Short-eared Owl	See range map 16

Owls Located in Much of Canada and U. S. (Except Southern States)	
Long-eared Owl	See range map 15
Saw-whet Owl	See range map 18

Owls Located Principally in the U. S. (Southward)	
Barn Owl	See range map 1
Screech Owl	See range map 2

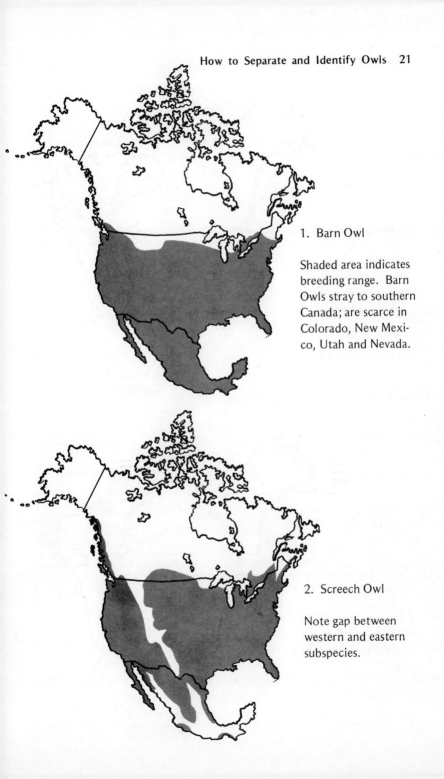

1. Barn Owl

Shaded area indicates breeding range. Barn Owls stray to southern Canada; are scarce in Colorado, New Mexico, Utah and Nevada.

2. Screech Owl

Note gap between western and eastern subspecies.

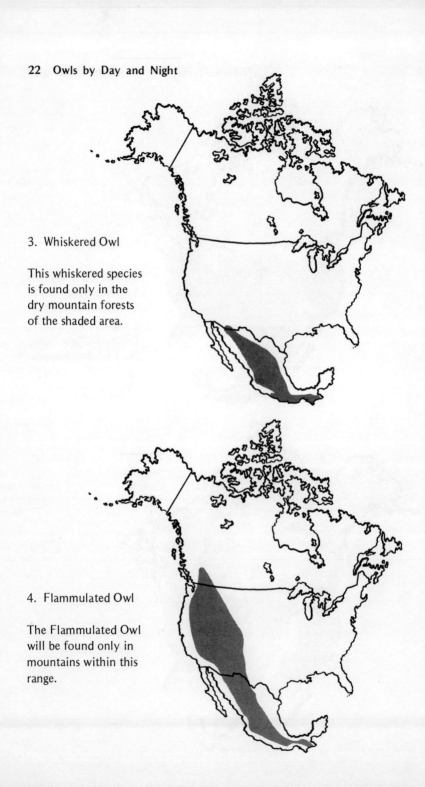

3. Whiskered Owl

This whiskered species
is found only in the
dry mountain forests
of the shaded area.

4. Flammulated Owl

The Flammulated Owl
will be found only in
mountains within this
range.

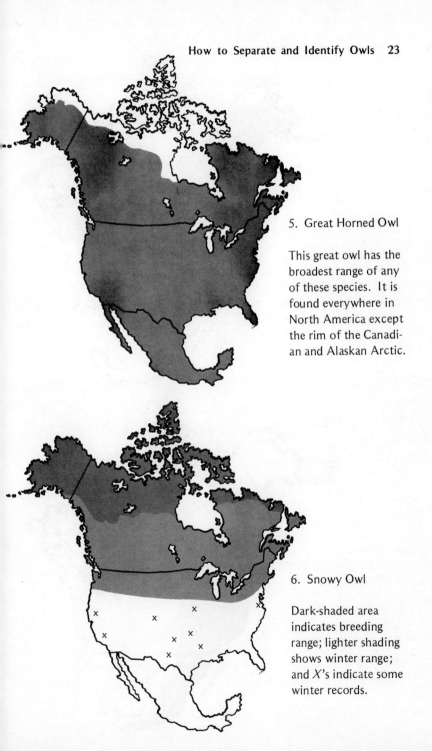

5. Great Horned Owl

This great owl has the broadest range of any of these species. It is found everywhere in North America except the rim of the Canadian and Alaskan Arctic.

6. Snowy Owl

Dark-shaded area indicates breeding range; lighter shading shows winter range; and X's indicate some winter records.

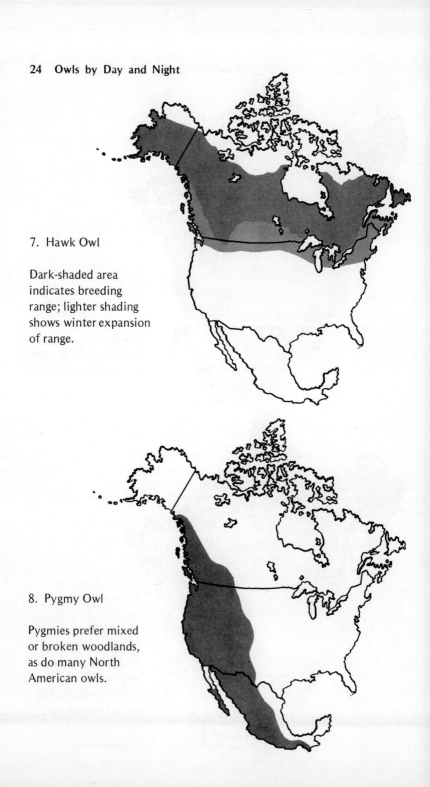

7. Hawk Owl

Dark-shaded area
indicates breeding
range; lighter shading
shows winter expansion
of range.

8. Pygmy Owl

Pygmies prefer mixed
or broken woodlands,
as do many North
American owls.

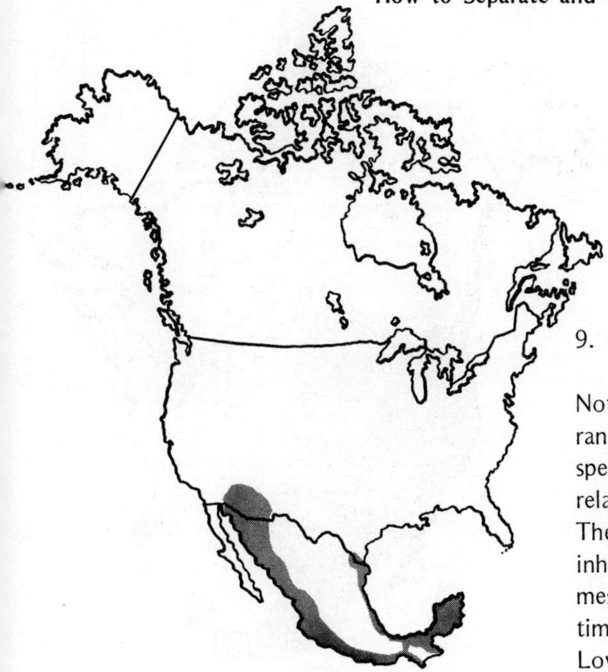

9. Ferruginous Owl

Note difference in range between this species and the closely related Pygmy Owl. The Ferruginous inhabits saguaro cacti, mesquite, or riparian timber areas of the Lower Sonoran zone.

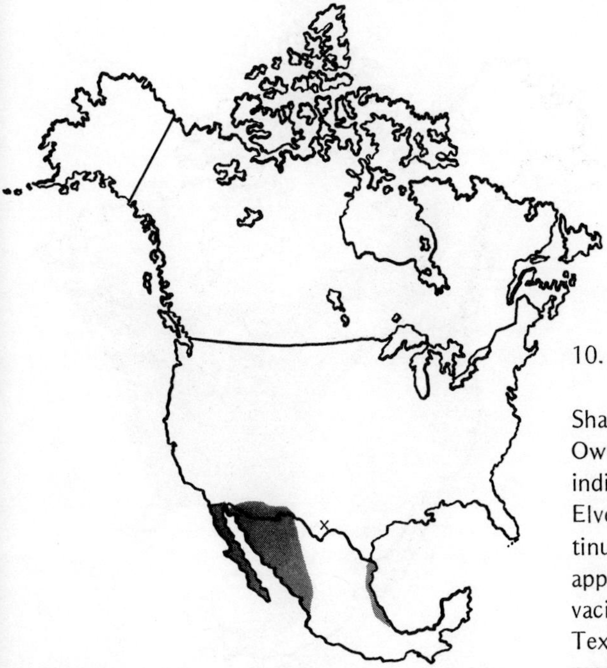

10. Elf Owl

Shaded area shows Elf Owl range; here X indicates the fact that Elves have a discontinuous territory, appearing also in the vacinity of Big Bend, Texas, during summer months.

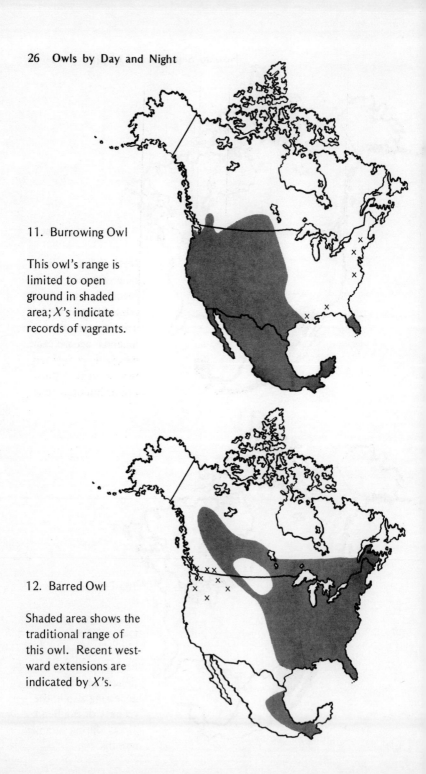

11. Burrowing Owl

This owl's range is limited to open ground in shaded area; *X*'s indicate records of vagrants.

12. Barred Owl

Shaded area shows the traditional range of this owl. Recent westward extensions are indicated by *X*'s.

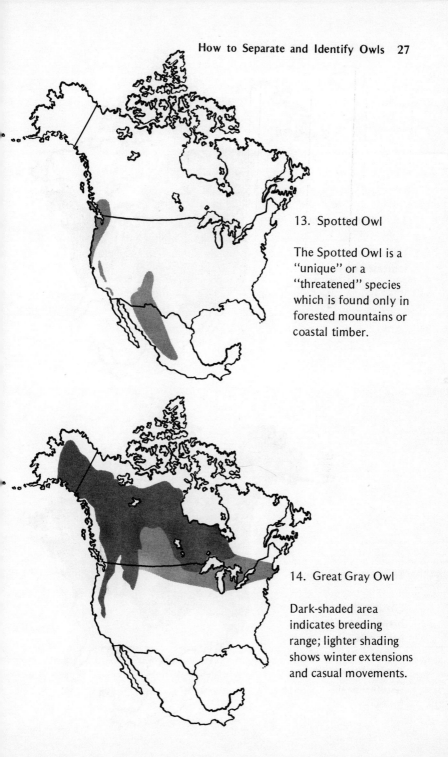

13. Spotted Owl

The Spotted Owl is a "unique" or a "threatened" species which is found only in forested mountains or coastal timber.

14. Great Gray Owl

Dark-shaded area indicates breeding range; lighter shading shows winter extensions and casual movements.

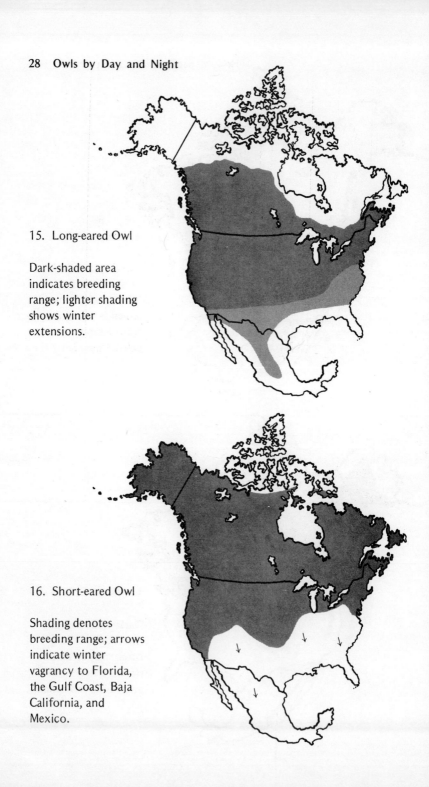

15. Long-eared Owl

Dark-shaded area
indicates breeding
range; lighter shading
shows winter
extensions.

16. Short-eared Owl

Shading denotes
breeding range; arrows
indicate winter
vagrancy to Florida,
the Gulf Coast, Baja
California, and
Mexico.

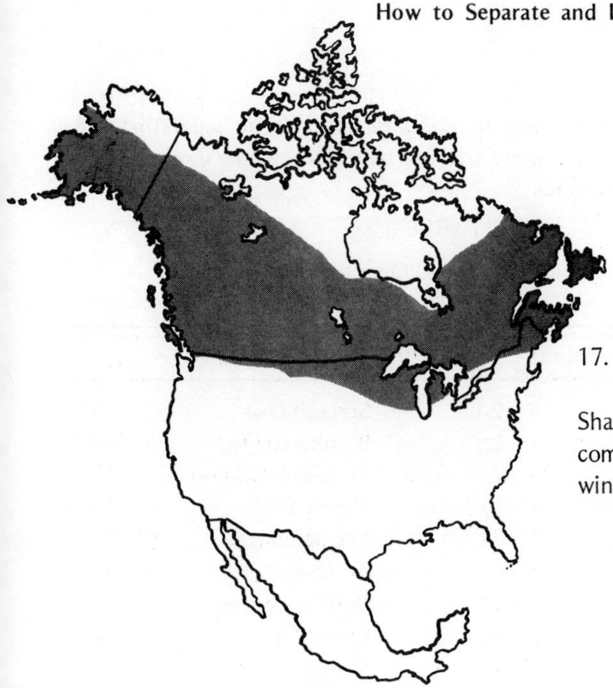

17. Boreal Owl

Shaded area shows combined summer-winter ranges.

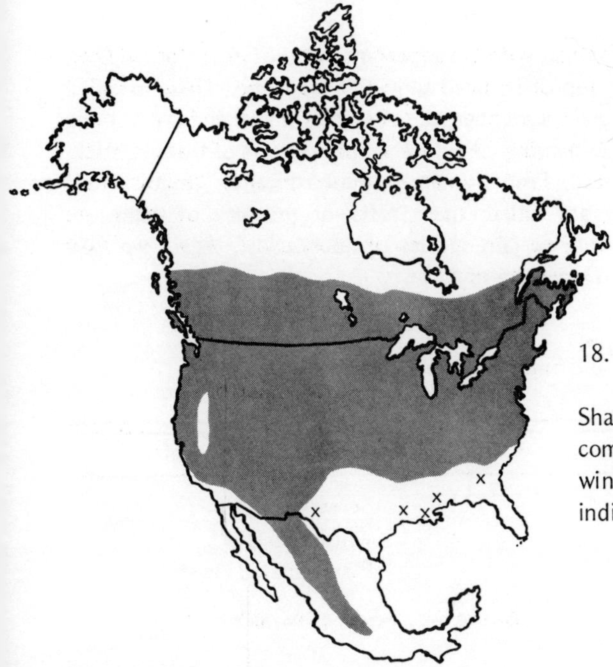

18. Saw-whet Owl

Shaded area shows combined summer-winter ranges; X's indicate winter strays.

Another very obvious division can be made by separating large and small owls. There is no overlap between the two groups, as evidenced by the next table.

TABLE 3

Large Owls and Small Owls by Length

Large (13 inches or more)		Small (12 inches or less)	
Barn Owl	14"--20"	Screech Owl	7"--10"
Great Horned Owl	18"--25"	Whiskered Owl	6.5"--8"
Snowy Owl	20"--28"	Flammulated Owl	6"--7"
Hawk Owl	14"--17"	Pygmy Owl	6"--7.5"
Barred Owl	16"--24"	Ferruginous Owl	6"--7"
Spotted Owl	16"--19"	Elf Owl	5"--6"
Great Gray Owl	24"--33"	Burrowing Owl	8.5"--11"
Long-eared Owl	13"--16"	Boreal Owl	8"--12"
Short-eared Owl	13"--17"	Saw-whet Owl	7"--8.5"

Everyone is familiar with the appearance of the Great Horned Owl, which has tufts on top of its head to justify the name. These so-called "horns" or "ears" grace a number of owl species, and they have nothing whatever to do with hearing—they are simply clusters of feathers sticking up above the head. Properly named, these are called "plumicorns," but whatever they are called, these tufts—or the lack of them—are handy for recognizing certain species of adult owls. Again we may divide the table into large and small owls.

TABLE 4

Large and Small Owls With and Without Tufts

Large Owls With Tufts	Small Owls With Tufts
Great Horned Owl	Screech Owl
Long-eared Owl	Whiskered Owl*
Short-eared Owl	Flammulated Owl*

* Tufts are inconspicuous in these two owls, except on day perch.

TABLE 4 — *Continued*

Large Owls Without Tufts	Small Owls Without Tufts
Barn Owl	Pygmy Owl
Snowy Owl	Ferruginous Owl
Hawk Owl	Elf Owl
Barred Owl	Burrowing Owl
Spotted Owl	Boreal Owl
Great Gray Owl	Saw-whet Owl

If an observer is looking a perched owl in the face, he will probably notice whether the eyes are yellow, as they are in most species, or dark. Since there are fewer dark-eyed owls it is only necessary to list these, and again by size.

TABLE 5

Dark-eyed Owls

Large Dark-eyed Owls	Small Dark-eyed Owl
Barn Owl	Flammulated Owl
Barred Owl	
Spotted Owl	

HABITATS

We tend to think of owls as being woodland creatures, but that is by no means true of all owls, and a knowledge of which species are likely to be found in what habitat will help with identification.

TABLE 6

Owls by Habitat

Owls Found in Open Spaces	
Short-eared Owl	likes grassland and marshes
Burrowing Owl	prairies or scrubland
Snowy Owl	Arctic tundra, or beaches

TABLE 6 — *Continued*

Owl Limited to Dense Thickets in Pine-oak of Southwest	
Whiskered Owl	

Owls Found in Deserts	
Ferruginous Owl	mesquite or other thickets
Elf Owl	scrub, desert canyons, saguaro deserts

Owls Accepting Almost Any Habitat, Including Deserts	
Screech Owl	anyplace, including towns
Great Horned Owl	anyplace, except cities

Owls Preferring Woodland	
Barn Owl	woods, farms, towns with trees
Flammulated Owl	mountain forests of conifers
Hawk Owl	conifer forests
Pygmy Owl	open, mixed woods
Barred Owl	dense forests
Spotted Owl	dense forests of conifers
Great Gray Owl	dense forests of conifers
Long-eared Owl	open woods, thickets, juniper scrub
Boreal Owl	conifers or mixed forests
Saw-whet Owl	forest, or open woodland

By becoming familiar with the preceding tables, the reader will be able to reduce the potential species names for the bird seen to two or three possibilities at the most. Thereafter, the table separating calls (table 8, pp. 55-57) may be consulted and then, of course, color plates and text for final determination.

CHAPTER 2

RAPTORS

We tend to think of hawks, vultures, and owls together, sometimes under the rather old-fashioned name of "raptors," a word which simply indicates birds-of-prey in the grand sense—without the shrikes and lesser predators. Because of their mode of life, hawks and owls have very similar beaks and they use talons for grasping their prey. Both groups of birds play the same role in nature *vis-a-vis* small birds and mammals, but despite these similarities hawks and owls are not closely related to one another in terms of evolution. If one looks into a good field guide to the birds, it will be seen that the various families of hawks are placed at some distance from the two families of owls. Similarities between the two groups of birds are based mainly upon like methods of hunting and feeding.

The place of predators in nature has been one of the most difficult ideas for the public to grasp, partly because scientists themselves have not been certain and were thus in no position to pass along easily comprehensible explanations for species that kill warm-blooded creatures as a way of life. Bird predation is even more difficult to understand than that of the larger mammals. A mountain lion is said to kill only the weaker and older members of various game populations, particularly deer, and thus it is seen to keep the breeding herd in vigorous condition. That idea may not contain the whole truth, but at least it is a thought which is easy to comprehend. Owls, on the other hand, are known to kill various kinds of game birds and rabbits, the most popular of small game animals. In the past not too much consideration was given to the fact that they also ate destructive rodents, nor was much attention paid to the question of which owls ate what. *Owl* was a general concept applied to competitors who vied with men in hunting the same game, and if they reduced the numbers the human hunter might take, they were regarded as an "evil" to be killed. At that level of thinking, and unfortunately almost to the present time, certain states have offered bounties to anyone who would bring in owl scalps, with little concern as to which owls were killed. Therefore, not only were hunters encouraged to shoot owls as they passed across fields and woods, but any young boy needing pocket money was likely to spend his spare time killing owls for cash. It was as recently as October 16, 1965 that the last state, Pennsylvania, discontinued its bounty, and full Federal protection was granted to owls on March 10, 1972. However, further education will be necessary before the letter of that law is enforced in all of the states.

During the first half of the twentieth century, while states and counties were paying out bounties for dead owls, some states and the U. S. Government were also undertaking studies of owl diets, based upon pellet samples (see pp. 37-8). These studies showed that many owls were extremely useful because they ate mostly small mammals or insects, with other kinds of food playing a secondary role. Once this thought took hold, owls began to be rated by a score card classifying their "economic status," of which a report put out by the state of New York in 1914 is typical. It made analyses of the stomach contents of eight species of local owls and tabulated the results in columns of food items, after which the birds were scored as "beneficial" or "injurious." In that particular list all of the owls were classed as beneficial, except the Great Horned Owl which got an "injurious" rating, presumably because it scored high in the column: "Poultry or Game." No credit was given for the fact that this same owl was the lowest of any, except the Saw-whet Owl in the column headed "Other Birds," because destruction of songbirds was not a public issue at the time the report was made. There was of course a very good side to studies such as this, for they helped the public to realize that at least some owls were worth saving. On the other hand, they gave no hint of the role of owls in nature where man's economic interests were not at stake.

A thoughtful consideration of predatory birds with particular reference to owls, has two aspects, the first of which is the immediate economic result from some particular standpoint. If one is a farmer, a Barn Owl family, or two, in the outbuildings will do wonders in holding populations of mice to a minimum, while in orchards Screech Owls will do likewise, and in grainfields Short-eared Owls are a logical and workable alternative to poisoning rodents with chemicals dangerous to both man and wildlife. Beyond these domestic fields, however, live the much more numerous owls of various species which have little or nothing to do with the affairs of man, and some explanation of the role of owls as predators in the wild is needed.

Some years ago the Craigheads wrote a very thoughtful book which still makes most interesting reading.[1] The book aims to make a scientific assessment of the role of these predatory birds by studying food habits in conjunction with the size of various prey populations. If we add to their material a group of more recent studies, a number of certainties begin to appear, the first of which is that it is very hard to determine exactly how large the rodent population of any area is—and hence how much control a predator exerts upon it. Secondly, it appears that in many areas which have been studied, the rodents exist in an abundance beyond the numbers that can be altered significantly by hawk and owl predation. On the other hand, owls certainly do make local migrations to points where eruptions of small mammals have concentrated, and there they do have an effect in controlling the outbreak. The sum would seem to be that owls do have a limiting effect on the size of small mammal populations, but not one of elimination.

VALUE OF PREDATORS

Perhaps it is worthwhile to add a single, easily understood explanation of the value of predators as they function in nature and quite apart from any economic advantage, or lack of it, to man. In a complex situation any one explanation is of course too limited to give the whole truth, but this one may be useful in saving owl lives from thoughtless men. First of all, one may state a general principle: *a diversity of spe-*

1. Craighead, John J. and Frank C. Jr. *Hawks, Owls and Wildlife.* Stackpole, Harrisburg, Pa., 1956.

cies is desirable because it leads to stability of the community.[2]   By
"community" we mean every kind that lives and breathes and grows
together in one area, a totality of everything from the most minute
microorganism to the mightiest trees and from the smallest creeping
thing to the beasts and birds. In a diverse community adverse conditions affect only some parts of it; a shortage of one food item will discourage those kinds which use it, but things will remain normal for
other members, so the community as a whole can maintain its balance.
A good example of a community with no diversity would be a farm
with a single crop; if that freezes or parches it means a disasterous year.

Since each item in any environment is part of any number of
food chains, wide fluctuations in one part will affect many others. In
order to maintain diversity in a community it is necessary to prevent a
single species from monopolizing important requisites, either of food,
of holes in which to raise young, or of anything else that is essential and
in limited supply. Unfortunately there is a tendancy for one species,
which most efficiently exploits the particular habitat, to increase its
numbers to the point where it may completely overrun the place.

That is where the owls come in, if we take these birds as symbols
of predators in general. Predators tend to kill the most abundant and
thus most easily obtained prey, which in turn tends to reduce the numbers of that species, and at the same time it works to spare those kinds
which are fewer in number. As a result, both diversity and balance are
maintained. Scientists have applied the name of "top predator" to any
species which stands over a community, as the Great Horned Owl does,
and maintains both its diversity and stability by always feeding on the
most abundant prey species. We will find many examples of owls
following this pattern in the species accounts which accompany the
plates. That value is the major "why" of predatory owls.

PELLETS

Both hawks and owls have a peculiar way of digesting their food
which, because of the haste of these hunters, is likely to be swallowed
"feathers and all." Not only fur and feathers but also all of the bones,

---

2. For a general discussion of this topic see chapter 19, "Diversity and Stability"
in Peter W. Price, *Insect Ecology.* John Wiley, N. Y., 1975.

beaks, and claws are swallowed along with the meat. Then, instead of expelling this hard dross along with other waste, hawks and owls, and to a lesser extent some other birds as well, regurgitate this indigestible matter in the form of various sized pellets which are ejected through the mouth. Since hawks digest a good part of the bony material in their diets, hawk pellets differ from the solid agglomeration that one finds in owl pellets. If one has a resident Barn Owl, or if he knows the day perch of any species of owl, mounds of these pellets are likely to be found beneath the roosting place. It seems to be the usual course of events for each owl to eject two of these pellets each day: one being expelled in the field before night hunting begins, and the other at the roost, where it becomes an addition to a mounting pile of similar fur balls.

PELLETS OF REPRESENTATIVE OWLS: **A** Saw-whet; **B** Long-eared; **C** Barn **D** Snowy   (*Photo by Don & Esther Phillips*)

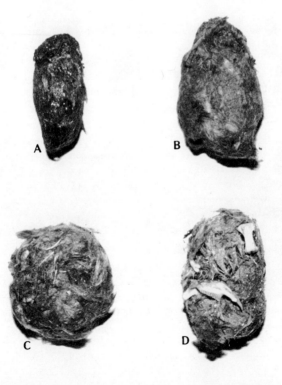

These owl pellets provide perfect evidence of what the owl has eaten during the past twelve hours. If the entire mound is dissected by a scientist, he can construct an informative and complete list of that owl's food items (Errington 1930). Many insects can be identified to at least the family level by the hard parts that remain, and almost all of the bird and mammal bones can be identified (see table 9, pp. 78-9). It will be a surprising pleasure to discover how many of the little mammal skulls can be identified without a specialist's help; what's more, pellets can be collected and examined by amateurs without doing any harm. Sometimes, when it is determined that the owl casting the pellets is of a species about which food information in your area is scarce, it will be worthwhile notifying some local biologist who may want to have the contents analyzed.

TYPICAL PELLET OF LONG-EARED OWL   Dissection shows the remains of meadow mouse (Microtus).   (*Photo by Don & Esther Phillips*)

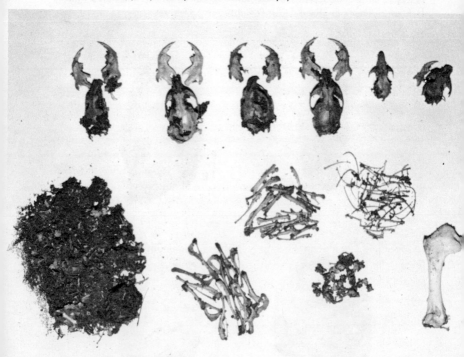

MOBBING

Because an owl is a major predator, it is feared by many birds which may become victims, and during nesting season the presence of some owls will greatly alarm songbirds concerned for their young. Responses to fear can take several forms: flight is an obvious one, while "freezing" is another of the common responses. However, attack is also a possible response and when a group of birds—often drawn from different species—engage in attacking a predator, the display is called *mobbing.*[3] Since nothing exists without a reason, it is presumed that mobbing reduces predation on the species which characteristically make such attacks, but that proposition has yet to be demonstrated by experiment. It might be noted that a number of birds will mob hawks as well as owls, but such events are more limited because hawks are less often down in the realm where smaller birds act out their affairs.

Not all owls are equally subject to mobbing. Those that spend their days sleeping in tree cavities are usually not around at the same time as their hecklers. The Great Horned Owl usually escapes attack. He seldom hunts small birds—bypassing them for larger creatures—and small birds seem to be aware of it. One of the prime targets for mobbing is the daylight-hunting Pygmy Owl which is not only present during the songbird's period of activity, but also specializes in feeding on small birds to the size of Downy Woodpeckers. For that reason anyone who can imitate the call of this small owl is frequently able to attract any number of alarmed little birds into his range of vision. One can also turn the same proposition around, and by listening to any abnormally excited scolding of songbirds probably find, after tracing the commotion to its source, some kind of owl being mobbed by a group of small or medium birds. The Screech Owl is usually not about by day, but if by some chance he is, the small birds are likely to mob him, as they will the diurnal Short-eared Owl. The Burrowing Owl, which is also seen by day, seems almost immune from these attacks, probably because these birds know this owl is not a danger to them.

Certain species of birds are particularly prone to initiating mob-

3. For experimental work on this topic, see S. A. Altman, "Avian Mobbing Behavior and Predator Recognition." *The Condor* 58: 241-49. 1956.

bing behavior. Among medium-sized birds, the jays take first place in both aggressiveness and frequency of attacks on owls. Among smaller birds, chickadees, warblers, titmice, bush-tits, sparrows, blackbirds, and hummingbirds seem to be particularly aggressive in initiating mobbing behavior, but once any attack has begun many other birds will join in by "contagion," a characteristic shared by both birds and humans. Different species of birds have their own manners which govern behavior during mobbing, with some, like the Wren-tit, cautiously remaining in dense growth and only approaching the owl closely if it is in a thicket. Blackbirds tend to alight in the same tree, or on the ground in front of the owl where they set up a terrible din of mass scolding. Jays and hummingbirds like to get right up to the owl's face. Hummingbirds will also buzz around and around the owl's head within an inch or two, interrupting this flight only to make occasional darting motions with their bills toward the owl's eyes—occasionally they mob a person in the same way, as I can attest.

It is a very curious fact that owls seem unlikely to respond to one of these mobbing attacks, even though a counter-attack would obviously send the little birds scurrying. Sometimes the owl will sit sleepily through the whole performance with no reaction at all, or it may move off into some thicker cover if the attackers are as large and persistent as jays are likely to be. Occasionally small birds will succeed in forcing the owl to leave their immediate territory whereupon the noisy throng follows for a short distance. There is seldom a report of an owl turning to sink his talons into one of the attackers. It is equally rare that any damage is done to the owl, though I have heard of a small Pygmy Owl which was killed by a flock of jays; and a local owlsman, Lynn Stafford (personal communication), has seen a flock of crows kill a Barn Owl by piercing its skull in several places.

CHAPTER 3
DAY AND NIGHT

We have seen a number of ways in which, as predators, hawks and owls are much alike and now we come to a fundamental difference: hawks hunt their prey by day, while owls are adapted to hunting by night. There are qualifications to this rule since individual owl species have modified the group habit for one reason or another and returned to daytime activities, but as a unit it is adaptation to the night which distinguishes these birds. There are a few other birds, such as the owl's relatives in the nighthawk-goatsucker family, which make their living in the shadows of dusk, but not in the dark of night. The flight-less Kiwis of New Zealand are true night feeders, while many ducks and shorebirds are active on nights graced with moonlight. These few aside, the fields and forests, once the sun has gone down, are left to the silent tracings of owls, or their night cries. All other birds have left the air for the security of some perch.

The chief and almost only purpose of the owl's nocturnal adaptations is better hunting; at night there is no competition from hawks or eagles while across the dark ground swarm the myriad rodents which hide by day—to say nothing of the nocturnal reptiles, amphibians and insects which come singly or in swarms. Since owls are so obviously specialized toward the night, we should take note of those which go about by day, and ask why they diverge again from their fellows. To begin with, most owls do a great deal of hunting at dusk or dawn, since prey is most active at that time and because the owl's particular combination of sight and hearing specializations functions best under conditions of dim light. Many owls will carry that a step further and hunt on cloudy afternoons when conditions approach those of a clear day at dusk.

Snowy Owls hunt by day during the Arctic summer, since the sun never sets then, leaving them no choice other than diurnal hunting. It may be noted with respect to this condition that the Snowy and Hawk owls have external ears of normal form, though larger than in most birds, which sets them apart from those nocturnal owls with specialized hearing; the Snowy Owl also lacks external ear flaps, but makes up for that by having highly developed visual powers. The Great Gray Owl is also perforce a daylight hunter at the northern edge of its range, but when flying to the south of the Arctic, it prefers to hunt at dusk or in darkness. The first basic exception to nocturnal adaptations is seen in the thoroughly diurnal Hawk Owl which hunts bogs and clearings in forests, much as do the hawks which this bird resembles in appearance as well as habits. There is no way of knowing whether this species is a relict from an age when owls were not yet denizens of the night, or whether it has reverted from owl to hawk patterns in response to some niche-opening which offered benefits.

The Short-eared Owl, which is found on grasslands and marshes all over North America, has become a specialist in late afternoon hunting and is thus also often seen by day. It patrols grassy areas in a flight which is held close to the ground in much the same manner as its predacious competitor, the Marsh Hawk—that hawk, it might be noted, has certain owllike features, such as a facial disc, perhaps for sound-gathering. These owls also hunt at dusk, and even at night, so they can be thought of as predators which simply like to get an early start in their quest for meadow mice and similar prey. If the Short-eared is a partially diurnal owl, the Burrowing Owl makes no distinction at all between night and day when it comes to gathering food. These droll owls pick up much of their food by scavenging on the ground for insects and other small creatures, or they may hunt from a perch from which they can observe the terrestrial life around them during the day.

Two small owls remain to be considered on the list of owls which go about by day. The very small Pygmy Owl and its counterpart the Ferruginous Owl are almost strictly diurnal hunters. These little predators have falconlike instincts and will attack small birds in flight, which is of necessity a daytime occupation. A number of diurnal insects, such as grasshoppers, are important in their diets, and among small mammals the chipmunk, which goes about by day, is a common food item. The Pygmy Owl is active at twilight but does not seem to hunt at night; however, as their hoots can be heard through the dark hours, courting must remain a nighttime activity. Diurnal habits in the cases of the Pygmy and Ferruginous owls is clearly a secondary specialization: day hunting was an open niche for a small predator with owl characteristics.

FINDING OWLS BY DAY AND NIGHT

This book was given its title to make a point about owls: not all are nightwatchers and even those species which are most nocturnal lead lives of interest around the clock, if we study them. There is a correlative point which applies to owl-watching, to the observer as well as the observed, and if this book begins to serve its purpose it will arouse the curiosity of those who have mostly watched ordinary birds. Observing owls is a rather special branch of bird study, one which begins by day and must extend into the dark hours as well. During the day one can often find nocturnal owls on their roosts since even those kinds which would prefer to hide in a tree cavity will often be forced to perch in the open. Their mottled plumage will make the owl inconspicuous against rough tree bark, especially if they sit where a limb joins the main trunk, but if the owl perches in the same spot daily there will be streaks of bird lime on the tree and ground; so watch for extensive droppings. Under any regular perch there will likely be a mound of owl pellets and while one is surveying the ground for these he can also listen for the many voices of small birds mobbing an owl with excited scolds. During this projected daylight search one will also rap the trunk of any tree which has woodpecker holes and from time to time the reward will be an owl face appearing in the opening. During the breeding season it is often possible to discover those owls that use open nests for raising their young and once that location is known the best of all watching, which may last for weeks, becomes possible.

Many nocturnal owls lead an active life late in the day as evening folds imperceptibly into dusk and darkness. The Whiskered Owl feeds in late afternoons while the Great Horned Owl likes to be on his hunting perch well before dark. The Elf Owl likes the moments of dusk because flying insects are most plentiful then and when a dark day simulates dusk, a nocturnal Barred Owl will sometimes be found hunting. But after all of these possibilities are taken into account, finding owls at night will still be a necessity. Night owls seem to call more on moonlit nights, both before and during the nesting season, and that is the best time for watching them. If there are no calls, or if one is looking for a particular species, it will be mandatory for the observer to do the calling, either by direct imitation or by using a tape recording. A useable tape can be made by re-recording a single call from the Peterson *Field Guide* records. Also, anyone can imitate mouse squeaks to elicit replies.

To locate the position of a calling owl, once there has been a response, cup both hands behind the ears and move the head back and forth like a scanning radar. Some small owls take special pains to conceal themselves by projecting calls with a ventriloquial effect, to fool predators, and in that case the bird will not be where it seems. It is thus better for two watchers to work together some fifty feet apart, so that by a kind of rude triangulation they may better fix the sound-source and flick on their lanterns. A three-celled flashlight will be needed for spotting the owl and to reflect its "eyeshine." The colors of eyeshine differ among various species and, from dark-eyed owls, this bright reflection is visible only if the beam is on the same level as the watcher's line of sight, for which reason a light is held alongside one's head. Owls seem not to associate a beam of light with danger and, therefore, one can often observe them for some time before the owl takes flight into outer darkness (Winter 1971).

TABLE 7

Owl Hunting Times

Day	Day or Night	Occasionally on Dark Days	Night
Snowy Owl	Burrowing Owl	Barred Owl	Barn Owl
Hawk Owl	Short-eared Owl	Boreal Owl	Screech Owl
Pygmy Owl	Great Gray Owl	Saw-whet Owl	Flammulated Owl
Ferruginous Owl	(by day in N.	Whiskered Owl	Great Horned Owl
	only, or in S.	(late afternoons)	Elf Owl
	if food-stressed)		Spotted Owl
			Long-eared Owl

From table 7 one can see at a glance the times of either day or night when owls may be abroad and that may suggest to the reader when he can expect to find a particular species. Still, however varied the times may be, owls are especially adapted to night hunting and we come next to their vision and hearing.

SIGHT

We think of most birds as the creatures which give sound and motion and meaning to daylight air because they are in peak activity during the bright early morning hours, but they become more subdued as the day wanes and by the time shadows become long, most birds begin to hunt for night roosts. The habits of owls controvert this pattern, since they have acquired special developments for leading lives that are opposite from other birds. While sight works best by daylight, hearing can be a kind of substitute for it in darkness and both may be modified to work together for special keenness at night. Nocturnal birds of any

OWLS HAVE EYELASHES   (*Photo by Jeffry Lapore*)

kind are an exception to the norm in which food is found by vision; hawks have exceptionally large and keen eyes for spotting prey at a distance and even the vulture uses sight as well as smell to find his food.   Since owls have reversed the ways of diurnal predators such as hawks and eagles, they at the same time had to adapt their vision to hunting in darkness.   Just how dark a darkness we will see shortly.   On minor points, the eyes are the opposite of most birds in that owls use the upper lid for closing the eye, reinforcing their half-human look. Most birds raise a lower lid for the same purpose and thus have a reptilian wink.   Owls also have eyelashes, which are bristles resembling the mammalian hair eyelash.

Both owls and hawks have eyes that are large and, although the part that we see may not look much larger than with other birds, some owls' eyes are equal in size to human eyes. It is not size alone, however, that gives the mock-human look.   Owl eyes are set frontally, as in man, but they are fixed in a bony socket with almost no extraocular muscles—hence the necessity of turning the entire head when following an object visually.   This eye socket is composed of fixed, bony plates which surround an elongated eye and make it immovable; but since an owl neck can be turned more than 180 degrees to either side, the owl can actually look directly backward.   Those owls which hunt at night have only rods and no cones in the retina.   That means a loss of color vision but an increase in nerve endings for visual acuity and light sensitivity (Marshall 1974).

An owl is not any wiser because of his frontal vision, and in fact birds such as crows are more acute than owls with respect to reasoning power, but frontally placed eyes are an important modification giving the bird a wide angle—70 degree field—of binocular vision and owls are able to improve their depth perception by moving their head away from the central plane.   At times, as any owl-watcher will recall, owls have a somewhat strange, drunken look.   That, however, has nothing to do with the hours they keep, but is due to the fact that each pupil can be operated independently to dilate or constrict (Marshall 1974).   The advantages of contracting one pupil while leaving the other expanded are many to a predator which hunts in varied light and shadow.   Owls searching for prey in the dusk will turn their head from side to side as they fly to cover more territory with their binocular vision.   At the same time they will also be scanning the ground with a hearing system which is locked together with the eyesight in a combination which exactly positions a small mouse or an insect, even in very dim light.

With this special type of visual adaptation it might be thought, as common opinion holds, that owls can actually see in the dark, but that thought is only a counterpart of the belief that owls are blind, or nearly so, in daylight. It is obvious that owls get along very well in what to the human eye is darkness, but that raises the question, "in how dark a darkness is the owl's vision useful, and how much of the owl's skill in darkness is due to hearing?" The classic experiments on owl vision were conducted by Dice in the late thirties and early forties, using three woodland owls—Barred, Long-eared and Barn owl—plus the open country and partly diurnal Burrowing Owl for a contrast (Dice, 1945). To eliminate the role of hearing, he used only freshly killed mice, placed in a room where the amount of darkness could be controlled. The results demonstrated that in light so dim as to be the merest fraction of that needed for human sight, an owl could see well enough to pick up its prey, if it were within six to ten feet of the mouse. There was, nevertheless, a lower limit of light below which the owl was entirely blind. The experiments further showed that the woodland owls had somewhat better vision in the dark than the partially diurnal Burrowing Owl, and that the latter often found its prey by diligently running back and forth on the ground, a habit which would be most useful in picking up nocturnal insects, frogs, and other small creatures.

Discussions relating to this topic bring up such questions as, "how dark is a night?" In answer, it can be said that not only a full moon, but even a quarter moon will provide ample light for a hunting owl in either winter or summer, if it is in the open. Woodland trees cast shadows which are denser in coniferous forests, while there may be no light at all on the ground beneath bushes or behind logs where mice make their runs. Heavy cloud cover can also make it too dark for an owl to see. There are some positive factors, however, which aid an owl's night vision on moonless but clear nights. Often there will be some auroral luminosity in the atmosphere which is caused by electrical disturbances. A regular feature is zodiacal light: a cone of faint light lying to the west after darkness falls, and to the east before daybreak. It is this addition to dim light which makes the dusk and the first hour of darkness, along with the corresponding hour before dawn, the favored hunting times for most owls. If they are successful then, there is no need to hunt through the darker hours.

If we have modified the thought that owls can see in complete darkness, what about the opposite assumption? Is an owl blind in daylight? Not in the least. Diurnal owls can pick insects from the air with a flycatcher's precision. Nocturnal owls, on the other hand, doze by day and are often seen on a perch showing no concern over an attacking swarm of small birds. Perhaps the eyes of a nocturnal owl will remain open in a seemingly vacant stare which presents the look of a blind man; however, this lack of response is due to the fact that the owl feels no danger, rather than faulty vision. Again, some species, such as the Boreal Owl, show no fear of man and at times will let him approach and pick them up. This has led to the superstition that they can't see an approaching man, which is not so; they have simply lived far away from man, for the most part, and have not learned to fear him. Probably all owls have better daytime vision than man has. Most likely, some owls see better in daylight than others do. The Snowy and the Hawk owls in particular have maintained better diurnal visual powers, and it may be true that some of the more strictly nocturnal owls are temporarily blinded by particularly bright sunlight when they come out of their tree cavities, but none of them are handicapped by notably poor daytime vision.

SILENCE, HEARING AND EARS

Not only has owl sight been highly modified so that owls can see in very dim light, but owl hearing has been modified along parallel lines, and it functions in total darkness. Acute hearing has another counterpart in specialized owl modifications: silence. If an owl's flight were accompanied by the whir and flutter of wings most of the value of its special vision and hearing would be lost. It is the unexpected presence of an owl, before the prey has time to freeze or hide, that makes its attack so effective. Unlike hawks, owls are slow flyers and lack the bulletlike approach of many hawks and falcons, so they need silence as well as darkness to cover their attack. The first adjustment toward silence comes from the degree of wing loading: owls have extremely large wings for their body weight, making them buoyant and able to fly deliberately and with a very slow flapping rate. This allows them to cover hunting territory in a leisurely fashion without the noise of rapidly flapping wings. Next, their feathers are soft-plumed, with many small filaments, and the barbs of the primaries or flight feathers are recurved at the tips, forming a series of soft hooklets. These lax connections between feather parts in conjunction with flutings on the leading edge of the wing, explain the perfectly silent flight of owls. Silence allows the owl to approach closely while the mouse or other prey runs over the leaves or grass making noises that the owl can pick up even in complete darkness. If these creatures heard the owl coming, they would freeze and become silent, which would necessitate visual locating.

DETAIL OF GREAT HORNED OWL FLIGHT FEATHER

At dusk or in the faint light of early darkness, hearing is at least as important as sight; therefore, nocturnal owls have special adaptations for both registering the most minute sound and for zeroing in on its source. The classic study of an owl's hearing ability was made using the Barn Owl (Payne 1962). Many farmers, or others with outbuildings, have long been aware of the ability of Barn Owls to take mice in such places even after the building has been shut up and the birds left in complete darkness. Obviously they do it by hearing the mouse run across the floor, but being able to hear a small sound is one thing, while being able to pounce on the exact spot is another.

The experimenter first eliminated the possibility that the owl used some kind of infra-red sensitivity based on the body heat of its prey. To demonstrate this point he first pulled a scrap of paper across the floor of a darkened room with a string. While the paper radiated no heat, the owl was able to pounce right on it in complete darkness. The next question to be answered was "why did the owl never miss?" After all, lunging at a sound in the dark is not in any obvious way a precision act and one would expect that sometimes the mark would be missed and that the mouse would escape. The first thing that the scientist found was that if all the frequencies above 8500 cycles per second were filtered out, then the owl *did* miss. That meant that its precision in striking the sound-source was dependent on the high frequency sounds which the owl was receiving. The investigator then surmised that the asymmetrical outer ears, or *conchae*, of the Barn Owl might affect the reception of these sounds.

BARN OWL WITH FACIAL DISC FEATHERS LIFTED EXPOSING EXTERNAL EAR

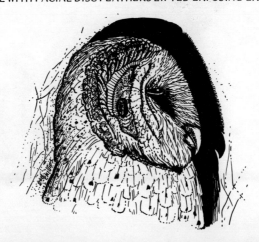

Barn Owls are not the only species to have these asymmetrical external ears, in which the *concha* on one side is placed higher than the line of sight, while that on the opposite side is lower [for details: (Kelso 1940)]. The Short-eared and Long-eared owls of the genus *Asio* are somewhat asymmetrical in ear arrangement, as are the three owls of the genus *Strix*, of which the best known is the Barred Owl. Additionally, the most extreme development of this characteristic is found in the Saw-whet and Boreal owls—where the skull is quite distorted to achieve this ear arrangement. Hence we can assume that the function is not at all limited to Barn Owls, even though it was the only species used in the study. The results, without delving into technical details, showed that if an owl with this structure for hearing faced the sound and adjusted its head to receive a maximum intensity in each ear, its line of "sight" would be on target. It could then, while in flight, continue to orient its head to hear equal and maximum loudness in each ear and so arrive within minutes-of-angle of the sound-source, or mouse. Since each ear was registering on a different plane, one ear automatically corrected the other and prevented any deviation from the true path to the prey. Then at the last moment the Barn Owl threw up its talons to the point where its line of sight would be, spread out each claw with two forward and two back and formed an oval trap within which the mouse victim was captured.

OWL SKULL SHOWING ASYMMETRICAL EAR OPENINGS   Some owls have highly modified skulls to accomodate the differential adjustment of ears for maximum reception of sounds from prey.

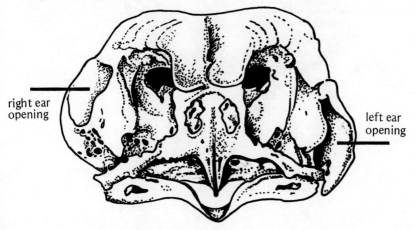

right ear
opening

left ear
opening

In this system any differences in reception due to incorrect orientation of the head would be amplified, with reception in one ear fading, while the other ear is always in an area of high reception where it can monitor the opposite. Though the experiments were carried out in complete darkness, it will be noted that they involved a line of "sight" which was correlated with the ears and that at the final moment the owl swung its talons out in front on this plane just at the instant of grasping. It is thus obvious that in dim light visual and auditory responses work in unison, day vision joining with night hearing in a combination perfected for dusk or dawn, but serving well in any light, or without it.

BOOMING POSTURE   Related to "Voice," this drawing shows typical posture of Great Horned Owl for booming out *hoos* to establish territory and attract a mate.

CHAPTER 4
VOICES

We have moved from the silence of owls in flight to their almost uncanny ability to register and act upon high-frequency sounds inaudible to humans. The next consideration is the multiplicity of sounds made by owls. These calls can scarcely be spoken of as "songs," but they are certainly a voice. The owl's voice has two aspects, one of which is simple mechanics. The pitch of an owl's hoot, for example, depends upon the diameter of air passages, and that in turn depends on the size of the bird. Thus the Elf Owl's hoot is a little more than two octaves higher than the hoot of a male Great Horned Owl, while the Whiskered Owl has the same pitch as a Screech Owl. Sonagrams record technical information about bird voices in the form of a graph indicating cycles on the left column, versus second intervals across the bottom; one handy field guide even includes a few of these sonagrams for owls.[1] However, unless one is an expert in such things, a word description, imperfect though it may be, is much more helpful.

Owls have calls which are as different as mellow whistles are from bloodcurdling screams. Therefore it seems, at first glance, that one might easily separate owls by their voices. But that is only partly the case, for one must also take into account the fact that owl voices are, in addition to being mechanical sounds, segments of a language. Anyone who has read many of the printed syllables representing owl-calls

1. Robbins, C. S., B. Bruun, & H. S. Zim. *A Guide to Field Identification, Birds of North America.* Golden Press, N. Y., 1966.

in bird books knows that there is no end of disagreement on some of the calls and how these should be indicated. This doesn't mean that some observers have identified the wrong bird or have lost their wits in the dark, it is due to the fact that most owls have a variety of calls with which to speak to one another, to their young, or to the public at large.

When the biology of the Elf Owl, for example, was studied at length, it was found that this little owl has a dozen different voices (Ligon, J. D. 1968, pp. 15-18). One call by the male serves as a territorial proclamation and at the same time announces to any female nearby that there is a male in residence. When he has attracted a potential mate into the territory, he then uses a second song to coax her up closer to enter the nest cavity he has selected for their home. Not unexpectedly there are changes in both the volume and intensity of the song as the female approaches. After she complies and goes down into the nest, he follows her, still calling faintly.

The male Elf Owl also has a "flight song," perhaps to indicate just a feeling of well-being. Both sexes have copulatory calls. Since the male feeds his mate during the nesting period, she has a "station call" to indicate her position to the male. There are of course calls to scold and express disapproval, and the young have rasping food calls; but the pair also frequently engage in "dueting" which involves a round of both mates' voices.

With such a variety of things to be said it is no wonder that there can be some confusion in the phonetic transcriptions of owl voices. Nevertheless, one needs to know something about voices—since these and a flashlight are the only tools an owl-watcher has in the dark—and each species of owl does have a major call which can be distinguished. Probably the best way to separate these owl voices is to construct a table based upon elimination of unlikely species in any given area. First of all, one should learn the sounds of the three species which are most common and widespread: the Barn Owl, Screech Owl, and Great Horned Owl. For the purpose, the recordings made of bird songs such as the records which accompany *The Peterson Field Guide Series* (to the birds) will do very well for a start. Next, one should make inquiries of bird enthusiasts as to places where these species can be found locally and then make excursions to those areas at dusk. Where I live, there are resident Screech and Great Horned owls in the wooded hills just across the road; a Barn Owl resides just a few miles down the way; similar situations prevail all over the country. It takes only a few observations to fix these three birds and their calls in one's mind, although the Barn Owl is likely to make one wait quite some time before he reveals his calls, eventually he will make a rasping *karis-s-s-h!* as he passes overhead in the dark, or a discordant scream from a perch.

When these three owl voices are known, some of the other fifteen kinds can be eliminated on the basis of geography: there are seven species that the easterner will not find in his area in any season, while in the West, a Californian, for example, can eliminate six species. A reader can work this out for whatever region he calls home, and he can also take into account habitat, season, and perhaps the day versus night alternative.

TABLE 8

Major Calls

Three Predominant Species	
Barn Owl	Call: a high-pitched, rasping or hissing "snore," sometimes a scream, never a "hoot."
Screech Owl	Call: in the West, a series of hollow *hoo's*, running into a tremolo at end; in the East, a rising and falling wail, like the whinny of a horse. Transcribed as: *Oh-o-o-o that I had never been bor-r-r-n.*
Great Horned Owl	Call: a low, mellow *whoo, hu-hoo, whoo whoo.* (separated from Screech Owl by cadence and low pitch)
Three Species Found Geographically in Both East and West	
Long-eared Owl	Call: like a cat in distress. (bird nocturnal and secretive, in forest or broken woodland)

TABLE 8 – *Continued*

Short-eared Owl	Call: greets man with a *wak, wak, wak,* and a scolding note. (bird diurnal, readily seen, in open ground)
Saw-whet Owl	Calls: one, like repeated strokes of file against sawtooth; two, a soft, regular *quoo-ik*. Also, one note repeated 120-180 times per minute.

A Species Found Mainly in the East

Barred Owl	Call: hoots, but with longer phrase than Great Horned Owl. Often transcribed as: *Who cooks for you? Who cooks for you all?*

A Species Found in the West (or S. & C. Florida)

Burrowing Owl	Calls: evening and after dark: a two-syllable cooing, second note longer; similar in quality to Calif. Quail. During day a "chuck" call and a "rasp"–like static. (bird of open ground only; nocturnal and diurnal)

A Species of the West, and of Canada from the Great Lakes West and North

Great Gray Owl	Call: repeated booming *whoo's,* which trail off to a lower pitch. (rare in U. S.)

Three Strictly Western Species

Spotted Owl	Calls: a 4-hoot series: *hoo-hohoo-ho*; also a sharper, longer, barked hoot series. (nocturnal)

TABLE 8 — *Continued*

Flammulated Owl	Call: low hoot repeated steadily, with long intervals between notes. (nocturnal)
Pygmy Owl	Call: soft *hoo*, singly or staccato, with two seconds between notes; sometimes ending with a *cuk, cuk, cuk.* (diurnal)

Following these twelve most likely owls we come to two groups, each with three species; the first group found along the Canadian border, and the second along the Mexican boundary.

The Three Northern Species

Snowy Owl	Calls: hollow, booming hoots of mostly two notes, most often given by the male; when disturbed both sexes call: *kre, kre, kre, kre, kre*; also an intense whistle. Generally silent except in breeding season.
Hawk Owl	Calls: one, a hawklike screech—*ku—wee!* Two, a *rike, rike, rike!* Three, a *whir-u* when flying. (crosses into U. S. only in winter)
Boreal Owl	Call: like the *ting, ting, ting* of a bell, never a hoot. (Maine and Vermont north)

The Three Southern Species

Elf Owl	Call: a rapid, high-pitched yip: *whi-whi whi-whi;* or, *chewk-chewk-chewk.*
Ferruginous Owl	Call: monotonously repeated (10-60 figures) of *took* or *wuh.* (S. Arizona and lower Rio Grande)
Whiskered Owl	Call: low *boo's* in various patterns, often 3, pause, plus 1; or starts with couplet. (S. Arizona and S.W. New Mexico)

CHAPTER 5

NESTING AND EGGS

Some of the larger owls, such as the Great Horned Owl and the Long-eared Owl, nest in old abandoned crow or hawk nests high up in trees, while the Snowy and Short-eared owls nest right on the ground. The Burrowing Owl carries that a step farther and makes its home underground and the Barn Owl nests in buildings, but none of these sites is as typical for owls as are the tree-cavities selected by so many species for nesting, egg laying, and for rearing their young. Many of the nocturnal species also roost in cavities during the day, even during the non-nesting months of the year. Sometimes an old tree will rot out naturally

EXAMPLES OF NESTING SITES CHOSEN BY OWLS **Opposite top** Snowy Owl on barren tundra; **Opposite bottom** Great Horned using open end of tree stub; **Below** Great Gray utilizing juncture of trunk and limb for nest platform

leaving an expanded crevice or hole, but more often than not these nesting sites have to be provided by the hard work of some woodpecker or sapsucker. The latter birds often build a new home each year so there are extra and empty ones available, but only on a limited basis. Besides the woodpecker family, there are a number of other birds and small mammals which like the protection of a small cavity, so the supply is rather limited.

As a consequence, many birders keep a sharp eye for any tree cavities which show evidence of habitation—signs of wear around the entrance—and when they spot one of these, it is customary to pick up a stick and rap the trunk below smartly. One of the cavity dwelling birds may fly out in haste, but at times one may also see a sleepy or angry owl appear at the mouth of the hole. The rapping procedure is certainly a standard and legitimate one in bird observation, but the further step of reaching into the nest and disturbing it should be avoided by the casual owl observer. Owls have enough harassment from their enemies, without being disturbed by well-meaning friends. It is for this reason that I have said very little about owl eggs in the main text. In place of detailed notes on this feature, a general account is given here.

All owl eggs are some shade of white, except for the Spotted Owl's which are slightly off-white by comparison, and all are completely without spots of any kind. They are mostly oval in shape but differ in degree and differ vastly in size. For those with a further interest in the subject there is a natural color plate, drawn to scale by John Ridgeway, in Bendire's *Life Histories of North American Birds*, Plate XII. The plate is perfect for illustrating the variety of sizes and shapes of the eggs of different species, except for the Spotted and Pygmy owls. One feature which does not come across on the plate is the surface texture of the egg shells, which differs in the fineness or coarseness of grain and in the degree of glossiness. Bendire's accompanying text gives, along with general information on the owls, a complete account of each egg. These vary from the nearly round (27 x 23 mm) Elf Owl egg, to the large (57 x 45 mm) egg of the Snowy Owl, which is closer to the conventional egg-shape than are most of the others. State and regional bird books also give details of eggs for the owl species of the area, so it is suggested that the average reader satisfy further curiosity through these descriptions, rather than by disturbing a clutch of eggs he may find in nature. That seems but fair amends to make to the most persecuted of all birds.

CHAPTER 6

OWLS AND INDIANS

Anything which is abnormal calls for special attention, and anything which is the dead opposite of normal cries out doubly and loudly. The question asked is: "WHY?" If the normal works well, why is something that proceeds on the opposite principle around at all? The oldest answer to this question is that the deviant is some kind of sign to man; it is telling him something. Owls are very different from other birds because they go about by darkness, which is a time of fear, not only of the unknown, but of frightening sounds in the night as well. Owls contribute to the mysteries of the night with their portentous *whoo's*, some of which simply ask unanswered questions of the dark, repeatedly, while other owls add ghastly shrieks or meaningless gibberish. So, if owls are signs, it is not hard to guess what they will signify. Death and other evils which are the opposite of life will be one of their symbolic roles, but owls are complex birds and so one expects them to stand for more than one concept. For the Greeks one owl stood for wisdom, perhaps because of its calm and steady gaze.

The lore of owls as signs is world-wide in distribution, with a time span which goes back as far as records stretch, to the cave paintings of early man. We can only guess what the owl meant then, but we do know that he was there, watching from the walls of man's protected dwelling while the real owls hooted outside the cave entrance in the night. Since the owls of this book are those of North America, it will be useful to see something of how these same species were treated by the American Indians, who knew them well. It is a happy fact that the Indians, while recognizing the sinister side, did not limit their attention to that one facet. They saw owls in various ways, made allowance for the different species and for the complexity of behavior represented in these birds, with the result that OWL was, and remains, no single symbol for them.

It is known that the Great Horned and the Snowy owls had roles far back in prehistoric times, since leg bones and wing bones from these two species have been found as grave offerings in sites of the Mississippian culture in the states of Illinois and Michigan. One can guess that the meanings of these offerings are not unlike those that we will find in the modern Hidatsa Indians of the upper Missouri River. Since the Great Horned Owl is found throughout the continent and is imposingly large and fierce, it is not surprising that this owl stands at the center of much owl symbolism. He stands for "owlness" and for oppositeness, which a Snohomish myth from the Northwest explains in these terms: "The owl is below at night when it is daylight in the graves." The dead, of course, have a life just like ours except that it is on the underside of our flat earth. Down there the sun is shining while it is dark up here on this side. Illness is a harbinger of death and for the Jicarilla Apache two species of owls, along with the wild dogs, are involved in this opposition to health.

"At that moment Wolf, Coyote, Burrowing Owl, the Great Horned Owl cried out. All the sickness turned to these animals, for these are their animals, and cried then. The Sickness People had been around with these four. That is why they turned to these four animals."

It may seem like an odd choice to add the cheerful Burrowing Owl to the company of the evil ones, but it may be remembered that he does live in the underworld and can thus be expected to communicate with the dead through his subterranean tunnels. The same thought is used by the Hopi Indians of Arizona who identify the Burrowing Owl with their god of the dead, whose name is *Masau'u*. There is a twist in this case, however, as the same god tends to everything underground, including seeds, which makes him a divinity of crops as well. Since this ground owl is his symbol and "pet," the bird takes on a positive aspect.

The nearest settled neighbors of the Hopi are the similar Pueblo Indians of Zuni, New Mexico, who have a most favorable attitude toward the Burrowing Owl, calling him in their tales "the priest of the prairie dogs."

The Gosiutes of the Utah-Nevada border have a "how-it-came-to-be" story concerning Owl; his wife; Skunk; and Badger. While the kind of owl is unspecified, it is well known to those who live with nature that the Great Horned Owl eats skunks with no regard for the scent gland or its effect upon the predator so *that* is the likely species. According to the story, Owl went hunting, killed a fat rabbit and ate all of the best pieces, leaving only the worthless parts for his wife. She seeks revenge by contriving to have him stomp on the ground near the fire, where she has driven the rabbit bones into the earth. The bones enter his feet and Owl becomes too sick to hunt, so he sends his wife to Badger to ask him to hunt for them. Badger replies: "My brother *Mum-pich* (Owl) is a bad man; he lives by himself, and sings songs which we do not understand; he is a sorcerer; let him die." Next Owl sends her to Skunk, who refuses her aid for the same reason.

Skunk's mother, who had been watching nearby, implies that he has done wrong, angering Skunk who sniffs the air and looks around; "I smell something." Next he accuses his whole family of smelling and throws himself into a fit of anger, but soon realizes the cause. Owl has died and he has refused to give Owl's wife any food: "This stench comes because I have treated the widow badly." The Owl widow is of course just as much of a sorcerer as her husband was, so she tricks Skunk with some unreal bighorn sheep and when he realizes what she has done, his vexation is boundless. "His anger increased so much that he began to emit a terrible odor which spread in a great cloud over the country until at last it overtook the fugitive woman and child (Owl's wife and child) and killed them." Badger brings Owl's wife and child back to life again and the council eventually decides that Owl's elder brother, Hawk, will feed the Owl-woman and teach her son to hunt with arrows.

That story tells us the origin of Skunk's vile smell and that hawks and owls are more compatible than skunks and owls, facts which are certainly true, but it does not relate the owl to any Indian ceremonialism. For an important connection of that nature we can turn to the Hidatsa of North Dakota where two owls figure importantly in their myths and ceremonies. "Big Owl," who is also called "Speckled Owl," is a Keeper-of-Game spirit. Both the size indicated and the spots would fit the Snowy Owl and since the nearby Mandan Indians definitely indicate a similar role for that species of owl, we may assume that the connection is correct. The companion of Big Owl is Little Owl, who in some respects is a servant, but nevertheless also an important spirit.

Big Owl controls the buffalo, which are kept by him for a part of the year inside a great butte which is geographically an actual place, called Killdeer Butte. One day a warrior who was returning home stopped to cut down a tree growing along the banks of the Missouri River, but Big Owl spoke to him from the limbs of this tree, saying: "This valley is known as Owl Valley. You can make a buffalo corral

here. I will give you a ceremony called Earthnaming. When you perform the rites the other spirits will teach you the songs and what things to use with the Earth medicines. . . ." Owl is thus a superior of the "singers," those priests or shamans who keep and tell the myths which support ceremonies, and he directly controls the major game animals. This account continues, "the thirty women helped him build the buffalo corral and they took many buffaloes, tanning the hides and curing the meat."

Among these same people the Burrowing Owl was a protective spirit for brave warriors. One narrative of an actual engagement with the Sioux puts the matter succinctly: "After a while, one of the Hidatsa would go out of the fort, shoot an enemy, and run back. Just as he went out, a Prairie Dog Owl flew above him and the others knew that he was not shot because this bird was his god." Because of the guardian role, owl feathers were always worn by members of the Dog Society, a warrior group, and rattles had coverings of owl skins since these would frighten off enemies of the Hidatsa.

Arrows used for hunting or war derive their power from large hunting birds, such as the eagles, hawks, and owls whose beaks and talons can rip or penetrate flesh just as spears and arrows do. Among owls, the Great Horned Owl is seen to be the most powerful hunter or warrior, so he joins with the eagles and hawks to form the *thunderbirds*, those mythical creatures with flint projectiles for feathers. These birds are, in one role, patrons of men designated as stone-flakers, who make sacred arrows for ceremonies. For everyone, Owl, who goes about by night, has a great knowledge of what goes on under the cloak of darkness, and sometimes that can be very useful. The Taos Indians of northern New Mexico, when on an expedition, consider the voice of an owl at night as a warning of impending attack and if prudence demands they will then sneak off under cover of darkness. In the same area, Indians at one time fletched their arrows with owl feathers for silent flight.

Any creature which goes around silently in the dark is likely to have some doubtful intent, else why would it simulate the noiseless progress of ghosts and witches. But any number of owls have been associated with ghosts, not because of silence but because of their strangling noises, weird shrieks and horrid cries. The Pima Indians rightly picked out the Barn Owl as the species inhabited by a ghost, as he makes all of these uncanny sounds. Sorcerers are even more dangerous than ghosts and they too travel at night, often in the form of an owl. Among the Pueblo Indians there are a number of stories, seriously taken, which tell of wives who are also witches.

At night, when her husband is asleep, one such story tells, a witch-wife takes out her normal eyes and replaces them with a pair of owl eyes in order to travel to the gathering place of witches. Her fellows there are ordinary people and likely well known by daylight, but by night and for evil ends they take the forms of coyotes, crows, or most often: owls. In a story told by the Cochiti, a hunter is overtaken by darkness while traveling through a rocky arroyo. Soon owls and crows begin to alight in the trees nearby and then transform themselves into persons. These approach a rock which opens on command and into the cave stream the witches, among whom the hunter recognizes his own wife. He rushes home only to find her bed empty and her natural eyes hidden away in a jar. The husband then makes these eyes unuseable by soaking them in urine, and when he returns home after hunting on the following day he finds his wife sitting in the dark with her face concealed—with her natural eyes useless she is staring at him through her owl eyes.

While Owl sees things unfit for human sight, that is but one aspect of his nature and he has more. For the Hopi the Great Horned Owl on the one side represents the dark of the nether world, below. He can also stand for darkness gathering in the sky above, when the clouds of summer gather around the villages to bring rain. But, since Owl is always ambiguous, he may on the contrary frighten and drive away the little birds of summer who take the clouds along with them, and in that instance Owl is a bringer of drought. More generally, Horned Owl brings the heat of summer which is good for Hopi crops, and of course the real owls who talk on the summer mesas rid the corn or squash fields of their rodent pests.   Hence the bird's ceremonial representative, the Horned Owl Kachina, is a benign fertility spirit.

These glimpses of the ways owls were seen by members of a few American Indian tribes show the complexity of New World owl representations. There is not simply the symbol of evil so often found in Old World legend, but rather a diversity of attitudes. Our native owls are seen to stand for a number of forces in nature and the life of man. Some of these are evil, other forces are ambiguous with respect to man, while many are supportive of man's quests, whether for game or crops or for protection in war. The lesson here for those of us who are non-Indian, but nevertheless within the North American heritage, is that the diversity which we find is worth preserving. We can likewise learn to study the diversity of owls and to ponder their separate meanings.

PART II

CHARACTERISTICS OF SPECIFIC OWLS

CHAPTER 7

THE BARN OWL FAMILY

The first owl to be considered in this section has a family all to itself in North America: the family **Tytonidae**, to which our Barn Owl belongs. All of the other owls in this book belong to a second family, **Strigidae** or the "typical owls." The common name for this second family implies that there is something very different about the Barn Owl and its relatives which sets them apart, and in fact this family has diverged considerably from all the others. The Barn Owl of this first family is nearly world-wide in distribution, while the remaining species of the ten member family are found from India to Australia, or in southern Africa and Madagascar, with one species occupying both the Indo-Australian and southern African regions.

Most members of the family **Tytonidae** are characterized by the heart-shaped facial disc which has given them the second common name of "monkey-faced" owls. A second feature of the family is the small dark eyes, which is in contrast to the often large and yellow eyes (with the three exceptions noted in table 5) of the typical owl family. Most members of the Barn Owl family lack the ear tufts or feathered horns, which are called ears, but have nothing to do with hearing; the actual hearing ears of owls in this family are very highly developed as explained in Part I, Chapter 3.

One of the technical differences between the two families can be seen if one happens to pick up an injured Barn Owl: the middle claw has a serrated plate along its inner edge. These serrations form a very delicate comb which these owls use to clean their feathers. A second technical characteristic separating the two families is internal, but I can always remember it because of an experience I had. The difference relates to the breastbones in the two families and, as I like to see such things for myself, I acquired two deceased owls from an animal shelter. The workers had tried to save the lives of these owls, which had been wounded. There was no luck for them, but there was for me. The first of these specimens was a Barn Owl, while to represent the typical owl family there was a Long-eared Owl. These were skinned out as well as possible, then, to let insects and weather finish the job of picking the bones clean, I hung each by a wire among the leaves of an apple tree where they were quite inconspicuous. A month or so later, after the season had turned, a Spanish-speaking friend was helping in the garden, where he was most able, but he spoke no English and my Spanish is for books, not speech. At some point in the afternoon he called me over to the now bare apple tree with a torrent of words, cackling laughter, and a concerned quizzical expression. Having arrived under the tree, he jumped up-and-down, gesticulating wildly in the direction of the two dangling owl skeletons.

I would have liked to have said at that moment, "well, you see, that skeleton on the left is a Barn Owl and the outer margin of its breastbone is entire—not a notch in it—just like the breastbone of a chicken. Now this one on the right, it belongs to the typical owl family and if you look at the sternum, or breastbone, you will see that it is deeply notched from the rear edge (see illustration on next page). That's how to tell the two families apart." But I couldn't say that and I could tell by his expression that he was not likely to believe anything that I might tell him about why I hung little skeletons in apple trees, so I mumbled something about *lechuza* or owl, which probably made him even more suspicious, and hoped that he assumed they were hung up there to ward off gophers and their spirits.

So it is probably best to let such characteristics pass unnoticed and separate the two owl families by the heart-shaped facial disc of the Barn Owl, which is emphasized by an elongated skull and beak, as opposed to the round faces of typical owls. If one needs further means for identification, the legs of the Barn Owl are longer and can be seen more readily than other owls' legs, with the exception of the Burrowing Owl's.

SKELETAL STRUCTURE OF TYPICAL OWL FAMILY (**Strigidae**)

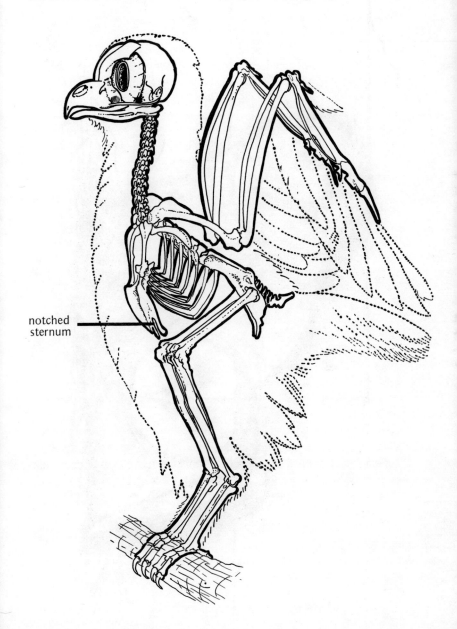

notched
sternum

BARN OWL *(Tyto alba)*

Specifics: Length: 14 to 20". Wingspread: 40 to 47". Weight: 11 to 21 ozs.

Range: world-wide (see N. A. distribution map 1, p. 21).

The Barn Owls which live in our steeples and barns across the United States, or in cavities of remotely placed western cliffs, are the identical species with those found in almost all countries of the world, even to the southern tips of Africa, Australia, and South America. This species is absent only from northern lands in Canada, Alaska, Norway, Sweden, Siberia, and the zoologically-odd island of New Zealand. It is a thoroughly adaptable species, equally at home in the tropics or in temperate countries. Of our two other common and well-known owls, the Screech Owl is confined to North America and the Great Horned Owl to the Western Hemisphere, although both of these have related fellow species in the Old World.

Opposite BARN OWLETS

Since Barn Owls belong to a separate family, they don't resemble other owls closely, as we have seen. To begin with, a Barn Owl has a very large head to go with its crow-sized body, and as both its wings and legs are long the impression given is that of a bird with a slightly shrunken body. The facial disc of the Barn Owl differs from other owls in being heart-shaped, or "monkey-faced" as common speech has it. In the middle of this white heart is an impressive and somewhat elongated beak. The upperside of this bird is a tawny golden with gray, while the underparts are white or pale cinnamon, but there are darker and lighter birds, with the females always slightly darker than the corresponding males. The upperside is flecked with both brown and white spots, while the underside is lightly dusted with dusky or black flecks.

The Barn Owl is probably the most strictly nocturnal of all our owl species, in part because by day—even a dark cloudy day—it may fall victim to the fierce Great Horned Owl. Therefore, it ventures out before dark only if the pressure of hungry nestlings drives it from safety. Because it thus conceals itself so perfectly by day, it is able to live in or near human habitations without being noticed. By preference it will also return to its daytime roost at least an hour before dawn. If the roosting place of a pair is known, a birder can wait for their appearance just before complete darkness falls, at which time a rather ghostly white presence will flap past with exaggerated wing beats and often, to begin with, a bobbing, indirect flight. Probably there will be two birds, unless the female is incubating, as they like to hunt in pairs. The flight of most owls is quiet but that of Barn Owls clothed in exceptionally soft feathers is absolutely noiseless—more so than the flight of a moth.

There are few places within the U. S. where one will not have at least the possibility of seeing a Barn Owl, and in many places they are quite abundant. These owls are occasionally seen in southern Canada, and in fact they even breed in southwestern British Columbia and southern Ontario and Quebec. Of the states along the border, only Montana seems to be without these owls. They are scarce in the Rocky Mountains; in Colorado they are infrequent summer residents with no breeding records. In New Mexico they are uncommon; but in Arizona, where badger burrows are one of the nesting sites used, the Barn Owl is widespread though of infrequent occurrence. There are but a few scattered records for Nevada, while in Utah this bird occurs only along the southern border.

The name "Barn Owl" suggests a building dweller and *that* the owl certainly is, when there is an opportunity. It will not only live inside a barn on a year-after-year basis, to the great benefit of the owner since this bird feeds almost entirely on rodents, but it will even accept a nesting box if one is provided, and that will make the welcome official. They have been known to roost and nest in a church steeple, not only in a small village, but in the center of a large city like Berkeley, California. The site in Berkeley gave them perfect safety from the depredations of hostile men, and at night they flew to the surrounding canyons and hills to hunt. If there are no such buildings for roosting and nesting, a concealed platform in the top of a palm tree or a blasted cypress will do. Barn Owls will also use holes in the sides of a cliff, pot-holes in arroyos, and, in barren country, any kind of crevice or cavern. Two extreme examples of nesting include those found at the bottom of a dry well in California and the nests frequently made in abandoned mine shafts in Arizona.

Barn Owls hunt over open country, avoiding heavy forests and high altitudes. They need the abundant rodent populations provided by grasslands, but they will equally take to cultivated fields such as those on which mice-filled alfalfa is grown. A careful study of their habits was made on the university grounds at Davis, California. There it was found that the hunting range of a pair of Barn Owls consisted of 165 acres, of which 25 acres were planted to trees and shrubs while another 125 acres were in grain and alfalfa. By sampling the pellets it was discovered that 95% of the food taken was composed of small rodents, as contrasted with only 2½% of small birds. These owls are so little involved in taking small birds that the latter seldom, if ever, mob Barn Owls as they do some other species. Also, it has been observed that these owls can live happily together with domestic pigeons in the same structure.

In the West, meadow mice and pocket gophers are favored foods, with other native rats, mice, and moles, as secondary items in their diet. In the same area they seldom take ground squirrels, which are diurnal and thus out of phase with the owl, but in the southern part of California where grass is scarce, wood rats are an important food item. Since this is the most entirely beneficial of all our owls and the species living nearest to man and thus susceptible to man's hostility, it seems worthwhile to present a table itemizing Barn Owl diets. Although the following figures are for the West, figures would be comparable in other parts of the country. This table shows both the economic value of the owl and how a predator maintains stability and diversity in a community by preying on the most abundant species in each area.

TABLE 9

Barn Owl Foods from Five Western Locations

Lava Beds, far N. California[1]		Soda Lake, NW Nevada[2]	
Meadow mice	68.0%	Kangaroo rats	58.0%
White-footed mice	21.6%	Pocket gophers	34.0%
Harvest mice	2.7%	Meadow mice	5.0%
Pocket mice	1.8%	Ground squirrels	3.0%
Birds, total	4.4%	Birds: 1 rail, 2 quail, 11 Brewer's	
(including 1.6% Savannah		Blackbirds	
Sparrows; others single)			

Davis, Central California[3]			
House mice	37.8%	If list to left is translated from	
Pocket gophers	25.8%	number of occurrences to total	
Meadow mice	14.7%	bulk weight, we get:	
White-footed mice	12.3%	Pocket gophers	16,400 grams
Harvest mice	2.5%	Meadow mice	4,400 grams
Norway rats	1.1%	House mice	4,250 grams
Birds, total	2.5%	White-footed mice	1,840 grams
(mostly Savannah Sparrows)		Birds, total	570 grams

1. Bond, *Condor*, February 1939, p. 60. These pellets had a small number of Horned Owl in the mix; mostly Barn Owl.
2. Alcorn, *Condor*, May 1942, p. 129.
3. Evans & Emlen, *Condor*, January 1947, p. 5.

TABLE 9 *(Continued)*

Berkeley, Central Coast of Calif.[4]		Coastal Los Angeles Co., of Calif.[5]	
Meadow mice	64.0%	Woodrats	64.5%
White-footed mice	14.0%	Norway rats	12.2%
Harvest mice	8.6%	Meadow mice	10.0%
Pocket gophers	4.8%	Pocket gophers	2.3%
Shrews	1.8%	Harvest mice	2.3%
Birds: none		Shrews	2.3%
Jerusalem crickets	5.6%	Birds (unspecified)	4.5%
		Jerusalem crickets	2.3%

It has already been mentioned that the Great Horned Owl is sometimes an enemy of the Barn Owl. In the past, when parts of the West were still in a primitive state, the Prairie Falcon was also a foe of this owl. Since my father was particularly interested in the ways of these falcons, and wrote articles on their habits, we spent many spring days observing them in the rolling wilderness of the inner Coast Range in central California. The hills were treeless, but in spring the grass was deep and rodents were abundant. Barn Owls nested there in pot-holes along the washes, just as the Prairie Falcon did. Once, an owl that we had probably frightened from its nest flapped up into the sunlight. Before it had reached the opposite cliff, a Prairie Falcon appeared above. There was a shrieking dive, the sound of impact. Then the air was filled with a little snowfall of owl feathers turning over and over again as they fluttered down the blue sky.

But even in former times the only serious enemy of the Barn Owl was man. As farming moved westward, the number of rodents increased and concentrated in the tilled fields, where some of them ate green growing things, others fed on grain, while gophers chomped away at the roots underground. Even as early as the turn of the century some farmers realized what a good ally they had in this owl. Barn Owls not

4. Foster, *Condor*, Sept. 1927, p. 246.
5. Cunningham, *Condor*, May 1960, p. 222.

only fill themselves with all the mice and gophers they can swallow during the night, but they also like to bring spare food back to the nest, making their roosts always something of a charnel house. That may not be tidy, but these owls certainly are helpful to the landlord.

One unusual characteristic of the Barn Owl is that it maintains a breeding capability throughout the year (Ames 1967). In the more southerly parts of its range the birds seem to be double-brooded. Other owls have a rather strictly limited breeding period and it benefits the Barn Owl to have a year-around-capability for mating in that they can take advantage of any particularly favorable food supply and fit the nesting season to it. Early broods have been reported for the month of January in southern California and for February in Texas; eggs are laid in April in Washington D. C., while there are July to December records for the state of New York. From three to seven eggs are laid and it takes some four months from egg laying to the fledgling stage. The male seems to help some with the incubation since the two sexes have been seen together on clutches of eggs. The nest may consist of nothing more than the bare earth or wood on which the eggs are laid, but frequently bits of fur from regurgitated pellets are found with the eggs.

The young are entirely white in the downy stage and the elongated beak and head is most notable then, which fits their feisty disposition: the whole group of young birds will hiss in chorus if their huddle is approached; they strike at anything, which may help discourage small intruders from the accessible nest.

Adult Barn Owls are somewhat apartment- or condominium-minded: they will let a second pair occupy the same quarters for nesting and, especially in the wintertime, these owls become quite gregarious. There are many reports of them gathering together in quarries and junkyards for communal roosting during the winter season. As a matter of fact, in southern Utah at least thirty birds were found occupying the same small natural cavern (Behle 1958, p. 52).

It is often very difficult to explain Barn Owl numbers in any given locality. In the central California foothills, for example, where gophers are endlessly abundant for food, it was found that only a few of these owls were present in a particular area, while 132 Horned Owls occupied the same fields (Fitch 1947).   Since the latter are known enemies of Barn Owls, it was assumed that the greater owls inhibited the presence of the lesser species.   In the same decade as that study another was underway in the Lava Beds—Tule Lake area of northeastern California and there it was found that during a single year 300 Barn Owls occupied the rugged cliffs, while there were only four pairs of Great Horned Owls (Bond 1939). Food for both was abundant during the year in question, so it was not a determining factor in the relative populations of the two species. The one difference in this area that seemed to favor the Barn Owl was the endless supply of holes and crevices in the lava cliffs which could be used for nesting and roosting, and with that protection they could apparently survive alongside the Great Horned Owl.

The Barn Owl offers a variety of calls, but never a "hoot." It has often been noted that this is the bird which should have been named "screech" owl.   When it flies overhead in the dark one will hear a *kar-r-r-r-ick*, or if the bird is alarmed it will utter a shrill, screeching cry of fright.   A clicking sound is also frequent, and then there are the haunted-house noises: a soft ascending wheezy cry, and if that won't do, a rasping snore which makes one think of strangulation—a prolonged *sksck*.   These sounds in the dark are very interesting, providing one is aware of their true source.

MALE BARN OWL PROTECTING YOUNG ADULTS   (*Photo by Don & Esther Phillips*)

CHAPTER 8
THE TYPICAL OWL FAMILY

On a world-wide basis, less than a dozen species of owls belong to the Barn Owl family. All of the other one hundred and twenty owls of the world belong to this second family, the **Strigidae.** These are called either the typical owls, or sometimes the true owls, but the last name implies that there is something "untrue" about the Barn Owls, and that is not quite the same thing as saying there is something "untypical" about the first family.

The easiest distinction to remember is that the typical owls have round, rather than heart-shaped, facial discs. A facial disc is the saucer-like, slightly concave area which appears to surround each eye, but it is actually an acoustic disc for bringing sounds to each ear. The disc is not so well developed in the Pygmy Owl, which has diurnal habits and thus less need for nocturnal adaptions. Members of the **Strigidae** all have the breastbone once or twice incised or notched on the hind margin. In addition, the inner toe, of the species in this family, is much shorter than the middle one. However, the only point one needs to remember is that if the owl does *not* have a "monkey-face," it must then belong to this family.

SCREECH OWL *(Otus asio)*

Specifics: Length: 7 to 10". Wingspread: 18 to 24". Weight: 4 to
8 ozs.

        Range: S. & W. rim of Canada; most of U. S. to Costa Rica
(see N. A. distribution map 2, p. 21).

The common Screech Owl is certainly the most abundant and familiar of all our owls, either large or small, and that status indicates the
success of this species: it thrives everywhere. In range it blankets most
of the 48 continental states—except for a narrow band along the Rockies—and much of Mexico; it barely touches southern Alaska and has a
narrow Canadian distribution along the U. S. border, up the entire
coast of British Columbia and parts of Ontario and Quebec. Almost
everyone knows this small squat owl with conspicuous ear tufts, yellow
eyes, and a disposition so fierce that it attracts immediate attention. In
the East it is the only small owl, except for the less common Saw-whet
Owl and the latter has no ear tufts. In the West there are two other
species of screech owls which are closely related and hard to distinguish
from it. The Whiskered Owl can't be separated in the field, but it is

limited to southern Arizona and New Mexico. The small Flammulated Owl is widespread in the pine forests of western mountains, but seldom seen. It is smaller than the Screech Owl, and can be readily distinguished from it by its dark, rather than yellow, eyes.

Screech Owls of the East indifferently inhabit woodlands or woodlots, or abandoned apple orchards where there are a few cavities for daytime roosting. These old farms have a variety of food in abundance for Screech Owls. While many kinds of owls either shun man or like to keep a respectable distance between themselves and human beings, this little owl is almost as willing as the Barn Owl to move into town, particularly if there are parks or college campuses to provide trees. Everywhere the Screech Owl lives, it seems to be a permanent resident, although some may do a little wandering in winter to search for better food opportunities.

Western Screech Owls likewise live in broken woodlands and they will move right into the suburbs of cities when these have scattered trees with woodpecker holes. The kind of trees growing around their homes is of no concern to these owls, as these may be alders, oaks, or coastal conifers and in the remote parts of the Great Basin, Screech Owls are common in the pinyon-juniper scrub. Furthermore, as a way of demonstrating their complete adaptability, these owls take up permanent residence in the open desert, providing there are cavities to use [(Miller & Miller 1951) and (Grinnell 1914, p. 128)]. In one type of desert these holes are in the giant cacti, in another they are in yucca. If there are streams or rivers, cottonwood trees and willows provide the roosting and nesting places. As a mark of the success of Screech Owls, they are more abundant in this bleak environment than are comparable daytime predators like American Kestrels, Roadrunners, and shrikes. When the food supply is adequate, male Screech Owls will maintain territories about a hundred yards apart, which become stretched to two or even four times that when the pickings are lean.

In addition to being adaptable to any type of environment, the Screech Owl has a second quality leading to its success as a species: except for vegetable matter, it is completely omnivorous. While these hunters are limited to the nighttime they are not choosy about which of its denizens they eat; whatever is there, anywhere, is perfectly all right with these little owls. They will take large insects, such as Cecropia moths or June beetles on the wing, but they also carefully inspect ground and foliage for caterpillars, cutworms, crickets, grasshoppers, or anything else. During the same foraging they will catch all kinds of mice, shrews, moles, rats and bats, and when it chances to find them, the diurnal chipmunks and squirrels also become victims. Then there are millipedes, spiders, snails, scorpions, salamanders, toads, frogs, lizards and snakes to be picked up. Small birds, and some not so small, also fall victims to these little owls. The kinds of birds taken, range from an abundance of sparrows and finches, through orioles and Star-

GRAY PHASE SCREECH OWL WITH BLUE JAY PREY   (*Photo by Don & Esther Phillips*)

lings, to pigeons, quail and grouse. The list of bird victims reads like a field guide to the passerine birds, with a number of other kinds added as well. Recent studies (Ross 1969) seem to support the view put forth by A. K. Fisher at the end of the past century, that the eastern Screech Owls capture small birds and rodents to a greater extent than their western counterparts. The prey listed for southern Arizona (Marshall 1957) consisted mostly of arthropods, while the same writer states (personal correspondence) that during nesting season Screech Owls specialize in feeding their young on small migrant passerine birds.

Screech Owls are not without enemies of their own, and as these owls are abundant, other bird and animal predators include them in their own diet, a danger which probably contributes to the existence of the various color forms found among these owls—since they need protective coloration. The cryptic, mottled pattern may be of a single shade, or birds in the same area may be found in two color forms as in the red and gray variants so notable in the East. On the western deserts these birds wear a very light coat which reflects the grays of shrubs against the dull whites of sand. In the Northwest they are a dark brown to match the shadows of dense forests. In the East the mottled gray form is marked on the underside with the "crawling ant" pattern which blends in with the trunks of trees to make them inconspicuous. There are a few night-hunting mammals like the raccoon which will eat owls, but the prime enemies of Screech Owls are hawks that hunt by day. Avian predators are color blind, so it has been surmised that these hawks cannot distinguish the red of the rufous form from the green of the broad-leaved trees in the eastern forests. Hence the red form of this owl is common in that area.

There is another important difference between the Screech Owl of the East and the one in the West: their voices are not at all alike. Voice has a very important role in evolution, since one main function is to act as a recognition mark between the sexes; it's a signal to the prospective mate that both owls belong to the same species. There are, after all, two other species of screech owls that look very much like this one, but they don't speak the same language. Thus the fact that the eastern and western subspecies of the common Screech Owl have different voices is taken to indicate that they are well along the way toward becoming separate species. It may also be noted here that the East and West range of the two does not entirely come together; there is a strange gap between them in southern Colorado and eastern New Mexico. However, the two subspecies have not entirely separated, since it is the primary song which differs, not the mating duet, so there could still be interbreeding if East and West should by chance meet.

The primary call of the eastern race has been compared to the whinny of a horse. It is a long cry which travels upward in pitch and then slowly falls, with a tremolo for the final third. This has often been transcribed as *OH-O-O-O that I had never been bor-r-r-r-n*. The wail may sometimes be followed by a *ho-ho-ho-ho*, or the latter may be called separately, but that is a much less frequent series. In the West the notes of the Screech Owl have been compared to a bouncing ball, sounding like a series of hollow whistles on one pitch with long intervals at first, then with the pace speeded up to a trill. There is not the rise and descending glide of the eastern subspecies' call. Actually, the very fine roll with which the call ends is only pronounced in the coastal areas and becomes fainter as one travels inland a good distance.

RED FORM SCREECH OWL ABOUT TO FLY FROM TREE CAVITY NEST   (*Photo by Don & Esther Phillips*)

Male and female Screech Owls engage in a duet in which the female may be distinguished by a voice a fourth higher in pitch and less mellow in tone. These owls also have a number of other calls, including an explosive bark while in flight and an alarm note which they use if a Great Horned Owl appears. One reason these little owls are so familiar to us is that there are few places where the calls, usually of more than one owl, cannot be heard as soon as darkness falls.

April is the preferred nesting month, whether in New England, Florida, or California and there are usually three to five eggs laid on the bare interior of some tree cavity. Toward man, these owls in either juvenile or adult stage show the combination of gentleness and ferocity that marks their nature. When sitting on her eggs, the female is usually willing to be picked up without protest, but woe to the man that approaches the nest at night when there are chicks. Any number of ornithologists have had beak and talons strike them on the head unexpectedly and hard enough to draw blood. What's more, the female will barely return to her perch, before launching another diving attack on the intruder. Within the gathering dusk these attacks are hard to repel, or dodge, as the owl can't be seen coming.

When orphans have been found and rescued, the chicks are at first friendly enough to make agreeable guests. Like bobcat young, they will play gently in a defense which involves lying on their backs and waving their clawed feet in simulated attack. But after a time the young grow more serious with beak and talons, revealing their highly aggressive nature which encourages them to attack birds larger than themselves, or other owls if need be for defense. Withal, and despite some songbird depredation, they are a pleasant owl to have in the neighborhood and a spring evening would not be nearly so fine were it not for the calls, more cheerful than ominous, with which these small owls fill the scented night.

I recall one experience, entirely on the gentle side, with this little owl. Many years ago, while working as a gardener in a small, hillside town that in summer was all children, dogs, wooded gardens (and at night housed nearly as many Screech Owls as raccoons), I was approached by a half dozen or more shouting children who said, "come see, we've found an owl!" Because these owls often sleep by day in full view if they are living in a protected environment, that was what I expected to find. But the wide-eyed Screech Owl these children led me to was crouched on the ground staring from a bed of mosses and ferns.

Since gardeners take care of creatures as well as plants in their realm, I approached slowly and reached down one hand. The owl hopped backward a foot or two, but had obviously injured one wing and soon submitted to being gently picked up. Let me add here that there is a mixed feeling as talons tighten about the index finger, but this "young-of-the-year" bird had no thoughts of aggression, and often injured animals or birds seem to sense when they are being helped rather than harmed.

I remember the noisy children's eyes being like the owl's then, while we thought of a good temporary home. This proved to be a high balcony with a railing supported by closely spaced uprights. It made a topless cage from which the bird could, hopefully, graduate upward and out. The injured wing was not broken but perhaps the muscles were bruised, for I believe it had been struck by a car coming downhill in the dark. Before long the children had found a cardboard carton for a house, a bowl of water, a perch, and of course any number of needless things like doll blankets. The same energy was then developed by the children in searching for insects under logs and rocks, and their enthusiasm for this hunt lasted through the following days. While the western Screech Owl is probably more insectivorous than its eastern counterpart, this one became entirely insectivorous, including spiders and such, for no one could turn up a mouse or even a lizard. Perhaps this owl still remembered being fed by his parents in that he seemed to relish having food laid before him; and when he clutched a grasshopper in his claws, then transferred it to his beak, the awe-struck audience watched the performance like a stage show. His night life was closed to all, but by day the owl dozed or ate and exercised his wings from time to time. By the end of a week he could flutter quite well and a few days later, so I was told, he flapped to the railing about dusk then plunged over in a long glide to a tree in the downhill garden next door. The following day we searched, but the owl was not to be found. It is true that this species has a tigerish disposition when hunting or nesting, but it certainly does show other moods.

WHISKERED OWL *(Otus trichopsis)*

Specifics: Length: 6.5 to 8". Wingspread: 16 to 20". Weight: 2.5 to 4.5 ozs.

Range: SE Arizona to Nicaragua (see N. A. distribution map 3, p. 22).

If one meets this small owl in the field, by chance, there is no visible way to tell it from the common Screech Owl despite the fact that it is always slightly smaller than whatever race of the Screech Owl inhabits the same district. The color of both is always gray in Arizona, although the Whiskered Owl has a red form farther south in Jalisco. One's eye can't distinguish the difference in body length, the slightly shorter wingspread, nor the somewhat coarser mottling in the Whiskered Owl pattern. The two species look so much alike that even for an expert there are no distinct recognition marks (Marshall 1967, p. 21). If one holds a museum specimen, however, it can be seen that the feet of the Whiskered Owl are smaller, in both length and diameter of the shanks, and the talons are shorter and weaker.

The "whiskers" which provide this owl with its common name are very hard to spot when bird-watching, and they are emphasized on Color Plate III to make the point. These whiskers derive from hairlike extensions of the outer feathers on the facial disc which give a halolike effect around the face. The common Screech Owl also has a few such whiskers, but they are shorter, limited in number, and so make the display of facial brush less prominent. If these were the only distinctions, the novice might just as well forget about the Whiskered Owl, but it *is* a very distinct species and just when similarities seem to make distinctions all but hopeless, a solution of complete simplicity appears — *voice.*

As was suggested in Chapter 1, the first move in identifying an owl is to correlate range. There are very few places within the U. S. boundary where this owl may be seen. All of these are in southeastern Arizona and in the small mountain ranges, such as the Santa Catalina, Huachucas, and Chiricahua; the Whiskered Owl is resident the year-around where it is found. More broadly, the range of this owl extends as far south as Nicaragua. In Arizona it lives in the Upper Sonoran zone of pine-oak woodland; but it is the white oaks which this bird prefers, or oaks and sycamores, and it is the bark of these oaks which its pattern closely matches. When the ranges of Whiskered and Screech owls overlap, the two kinds live in apparent harmony; the same is true when the third species of screech owl, the Flammulated, overlaps from higher elevations. The tolerance seems to be based on different food preferences and altitudes of living.

The distinction in voice mentioned is a simple one to remember: the call of the Screech Owl is a series of notes given with an accelerating tempo. In the territorial voice of the Whiskered Owl the trill does *not* accelerate, but consists of a cluster of notes with even intervals, though the pitch is similar. The call of the Whiskered Owl is like an evenly spaced message in Morse code, consisting of two dots and three dashes, delivered in groups of three, without pause, followed by a final "dash." If the male and female are dueting, the song becomes rhythmical, but it still lacks in acceleration. The voice of this owl, or an imitation of it, will usually bring a response, not from small birds but from other owls. The Whiskered Owl is the most pugnacious of all territorial birds in its area, so when the call is imitated these notes bring up other owls of the species to contest the claim. An aroused male will puff out his feathers and strut along, dragging his wings on the ground like a turkey gobbler, while making straight for the intruder. If the latter is a man, the little owl will generally let itself be picked up while continuing to hoot aggressively (Marshall 1957).

There are distinctions of habitat since the Whiskered Owl likes the dense foliage that is found among broad-leaved trees or in streamside groves, which also offer concealing thickets of leaves (Marshall 1957). In contrast, the Screech Owl likes the open woods of lower elevations and right on down to treeless deserts. Another distinction is that the Whiskered Owl will hunt in late afternoons even when these are bright, while its relative is almost entirely nocturnal. The elevations at which the two species overlap in Arizona is between 5300 and 6500 feet, but with each sticking to its preferred habitat within that zone. Above that elevation the next species, the Flammulated Owl, makes its home in the coniferous forest for the summer, and it too overlaps. The Whiskered and the Screech owl again differ in methods of feeding, although in this region both prefer small things such as insects, spiders and scorpions. Elsewhere, as we have seen, the Screech Owl has no such limitations on the diet. Here, the Screech Owl sits on a perch where he can watch the bare or grassy ground below for the small creatures on which he dives. The Whiskered Owl, on the other hand, is generally an aerial feeder during the summer months, taking moths, beetles and the like in flight, or it will gather caterpillars and spiders from the leaves and limbs of trees. In the winter, when insect food becomes scarce at that altitude, the Whiskered Owls take mole-crickets and scorpions from the ground, and there is but a single record of vertebrate prey—a mouse. A recent study determines that moths, in both the caterpillar and adult stages, along with some beetles, make up the main summer fare of this owl (Ross 1969, p. 322). At the same time it was found that the Whiskered Owl fragments its food to a much greater degree than either the Screech or the Flammulated owls.

By April the protective male has established a territory and called in a female to share his nest, which is usually an old woodpecker hole, but it may be only an open cavity where a sycamore branch has broken off. They use little lining for their nest, just soft compost made of debris and rotting wood, with perhaps a few leaves on which three or four globular eggs are laid. The clutch is complete by the end of April or in early May and hatching them is strictly a female matter, although the male brings food to her during this period. By mid-June there are young Whiskered Owls in the nest. These are a nondescript grayish brown on the back and the underside markings are quite different from those of the adult. In the young, the light undersurface feathers have a strong crosswise barring, while the adults have pencilings which run parallel to the feather shafts.

Since the range of this little owl is so limited in the U. S., it is odd that, for a few hundred elevational feet in those mountains of southern Arizona, the same spots may also be the home of the much more widely distributed Flammulated Owl, but only during the summer since that owl is migratory. A perfect distinction is that the Whiskered Owl has yellow eyes, while those of the neighbor species are a dark brown.

FLAMMULATED OWL *(Otus flammeolus)*

Specifics: Length: 6 to 7". Wingspread: 14 to 19". Weight: 1.5 to
2.5 ozs.*
Range: mountains of West, in summer (see N. A. distribution map 4, p. 22).

This third representative of the screech owls is as meek in attitude
as its larger relative is fierce, and it has taken a side path in the evolution
of owls to become something of a waif among them. Even the ponderosa pine forests are not private enough for the Flammulated Owl, since
it inhabits by preference those that have brush as well as great trees. It
keeps out of the way of other birds and does not like to fly in the open.
Even at night, it continues to travel through dense cover, and it feeds
in the manner of a flycatcher, catching insects in both beak and claws.
Not all of its mildness is due to its small size, as the Pygmy Owl is
likewise tiny but thinks big and acts grandly. Not so the Flammulated

* (from Marshall 1967; Johnson & Russell 1962.)

Owl, which only *looks* like a small Screech Owl. While its length is slightly shorter than either the Screech or Whiskered owls, its weight is hardly a puff with an average of an ounce and three quarters, while its bones and body have a fragile feeling to the touch. In *behavior* it is nothing like a Screech Owl, being as mild as that one is fierce.

The ear tufts of this little owl are much shorter than those of the Screech Owl, being about the same length as other feathers on its head. But the Flammulated Owl likes to be as inconspicuous as possible. The female, especially, can flatten down most of its feathers and when it does this, as when sleeping on a daytime perch, the ear tufts remain erect. In the Flammulated Owl the facial discs are a rusty brown speckled with black and, as has been said, its eyes are a very dark brown. Only the Barn, Spotted and Barred owls also have dark eyes, and they are all large owls. The general aspect of the bird's plumage is that of a weathered mottling of light and dusky on the back, while the underparts are a pale ashy color marked with a series of vertical stripes. Many specimens have enough rusty or red in the plumage to justify the "fiery" in the Latin name, but the amount is variable, increasing southwardly until in Mexico redder shades become common. Again, as in other screech owls, the young have gray, cross-barred plumage.

It is of no use to look for this sparrow-sized owl anywhere east of the Rockies, or if the season is winter anywhere at all within the U. S., for they are strictly migratory and leave the West of our country for southern climates. The summer breeding range of the Flammulated Owl extends from southern British Columbia southward through California, and from Idaho through Colorado and New Mexico to the Guadalupe Mountains of southwestern Texas, as well as throughout Arizona and southward to Guatemala.

For many years the Flammulated Owl was thought to be a very rare species, but this was appearance only and due to the fact that they are secretive, as well as strictly nocturnal, so they can only be located by their calls. This species of owl doesn't call when it first arrives in the nesting forests, but by the second half of May calls become increasingly common and vocal activity is at a peak in June. By calling up these owls through imitating their notes, Joe T. Marshall, Jr.

(Marshall 1939) and others discovered that in actual fact they are common birds in California. The same probably holds true for Oregon where there are still few records. One student estimates that Flammulated Owls may be the commonest owl, in season, in the central Sierra Nevada where in one area slightly more than two males of this species were found per hundred acres in yellow pine and brush habitat (Winter 1974). However, since they are absent in other suitable locations dominated by the same pines and brush, these owls may prefer to gather into loose colonies for the nesting season rather than scatter evenly throughout the Transition zone. If one travels anywhere in the mountainous west during the summer, there is always the possibility of spotting one of these owls, usually in the Transition zone, but probably the most certain place for finding them is on the South Rim of the Grand Canyon, at Park Headquarters, where they are the most abundant owl. Their stay in Arizona is from the end of March into early October. Flammulated Owls can also be found in the Flagstaff region among the yellow pines, and if one is continuing east across Arizona, the Navajo National Monument is another certain spot. There, anyone who camps overnight among the pinyon-pines and junipers can expect to hear the calls of these little owls in season, since they do most of their feeding at dusk and dawn, leaving the night free for hooting.

Most of the peculiarities of this owl are related to its insectivorous diet and the method used in taking its food. Migration, for example, becomes a necessity because the Flammulated Owl eats no small mammals or birds, and when the first frosts arrive in its mountainous summer home, the insects which provided much of its food are gone and the bird must head south to where frost comes seldom or not at all. During the summer in the north, it collects various crickets, grasshoppers, and scorpions from the ground, but much of its food is taken through aerial acrobatics. At its favored hunting times of dusk and dawn, it perches in some pine or fir, then flies with great speed into the open space between trees, swooping up abruptly to its next perch. During this dash it will capture, by use of either bill or claws, one or more of the flying insects. In the stomach of an owl from Oregon 60% of the contents consisted of moths, while 35% was made up of darkling and ground beetles. The food noted from Arizona is similar, but with even more things such as crane flies from the air and caterpillars and spiders from trees. [For a detailed analysis of these food items see: (Ross 1969).] When this food is no longer available here, Flammulated Owls retreat into Mexico and as far as Guatemala, where their life style can be continued through the winter. Migrating northward again in the spring may be a relict habit from Pleistocene days or it may be a retracing, in migration, of an earlier invasion path from the south.

A physical development related to its insect diet is the presently fragile bone structure: as there is no need for sinking talons into vertebrate prey, the leg bones are smaller than in the other two screech owls. In contrast, the equally small Pygmy Owl, which is nevertheless a ferocious predator of small mammals and birds, has maintained a stance of bone and muscle which is equivalent to a spring-steel trap. The unaggressive Flammulated Owl keeps out of the way as much as possible, but it does have one especial enemy in the Spotted Owl which inhabits conifer forests at similar elevations, although the latter has different specific habitat preferences. When a Spotted Owl speaks all of the Flammulated voices fall silent at once, as well they might since the Spotted Owl is a great foe of all three species of screech owls.

The Flammulated Owl, unlike the Whiskered Owl, is not aggressive about keeping other males of its own kind out of the territory and it is only when a song-perch is approached that this owl will protest. There may be as many as eighteen male owls of this species within an area two miles square, with each territory occupying an area of up to three hundred yards in diameter, but with many overlaps because of the tolerance of these owls. Once a pair bond has been established, both birds feed within their own territory. The nest hole is likely to be a surplus flicker or woodpecker cavity, with housekeeping set up in late May or early June. Females lay from two to four eggs with the smaller number being the most common. It might be noted here that the females of this species are even shyer than the males and are very seldom seen, even with diligent search. Nests are also hidden away very securely and are hardly ever discovered.

During the mating season the male will call all night with only short interruptions, as when he sees a hawk moth and pursues it at high speed—dusk and dawn are saved for more serious food collecting. The call of the male is a single hoot uttered at regular intervals of

from two to eight seconds, with notes of a deep pitch which are decep-
tively soft and far-carrying in character. The call also has a very strong
ventriloquial quality which makes the bird hard to locate, and he further
compounds the difficulty by keeping objects between himself and the
observer. The pitch is low in the male and higher as well as softer in the
female, who can also turn the call into a quavering cry. Sometimes the
male call is introduced by two short notes which are slightly lower than
the main call pitch. The mating song of the male is a two-part *boo-boot*
with the accent and volume on the second note, and as a warning or
worry call the *boot* is given alone. Very rarely there is also a *screech*.
Most of the male calling is done in the spring with moonlit nights
favored. In the summer they are relatively quiet. Night hooting may
commence again in the fall before the Flammulated Owl's departure.

It may have occurred to the reader that an owl which specializes
in yellow pine habitats, with only a few excursions into pinyon pines,
has had the misfortune to choose exactly the kind of woods that
loggers are likely to cut down. It is true that the two species of yellow
pine (ponderosa and Jeffry) have been leveled throughout extensive
areas of the West, but by good fortune the Flammulated Owl is able to
thrive in second growth pine forests, so long as the undergrowth is
there for concealment and insects are present for food. Since there is
unlikely to be a scarcity of moths, beetles, and grasshoppers, this tiny
dark-eyed owl is likely to continue spending summers in forests far to
the north of its winter home.

Don Phillips

GREAT HORNED OWL *(Bubo virginianus)*

Specifics: Length: 18 to 25". Wingspread: 35 to 55". Weight: 3 to 5 lbs.

Range: N. & S. America (see N. A. distribution map 5, p. 23).

One step and we have come from the meekest of all owls to the dominant owl of North America, from the very small to the very large, from a hunter of small insects to a top predator who will take a skunk or tomcat as readily as a mouse. The Great Horned Owl is the lord of forests, marshes, and brushland, who presides over his domains with an unmistakable and authoritative voice. This great owl has the broadest range of any of our species, being found everywhere on the continent except the rim of the Canadian and Alaskan Arctic. The only other owl which approaches that vast distribution is the Short-eared Owl, but that bird is very local and also migratory, so while it *may* be found over much of the continent, there are fewer places where it is often seen.

The Great Horned Owl is the dominant raptor by night, sharing this role by day with the Red-tailed Hawk or Red-shouldered Hawk. It can kill a Cooper's Hawk or a Marsh Hawk in the air if it so desires. In a Wisconsin-based study [(Orians and Kuhlman 1956) and see also (Errington 1932)] it was determined that the Great Horned Owl would tolerate a Red-tailed Hawk only at a distance of 350 to 700 yards of its nesting site. The basic truth, that the Horned Owl doesn't like any of these hawks near its nest, is certainly correct, but the distances will not always be that great. On a narrow peninsula between ocean and bay along the central California coast, a Great Horned Owl, Red-tailed Hawk, and a pair of Marsh Hawks live in crowded circumstances. The owl would not tolerate any of these near its nest during nesting season, but they seem to have arranged, somehow, to all live in a narrow compass. Red-tails and Horned Owls do compete for nesting sites and as the owl builds no nest of its own, it must appropriate large nests built by other birds, often by this same hawk. One observer watched contests for nests and sites between this species of hawk and the owl and noted that out of eleven such confrontations the hawks lost nine times and the owls only twice. Clearly this owl commands the air.

Most other owls give the Great Horned a very wide berth and although the Snowy and Great Gray owls may look larger, they are not as powerful and will avoid their fierce relative. There is terrible power in the beak and in the talons of the Great Horned Owl. The talons will not only pierce through the flesh and into the bony skeleton of rabbits— or a fighting skunk—but after they are sunk in to the hilt the talons lock in place. The grip is so solid that in one instance a scientist had to cut the tendons of the owl's legs before he could break the mighty hold and release the prey. The powerful beak comes into play as soon as the talons have fixed a victim, and this owl can rip the wings from a Marsh Hawk taken in mid-air as easily as some other owls remove moth wings from their prey. The Spotted Owl of the West is so thoroughly afraid of this predator that one of the requirements for its own habitation is that there are no Horned Owls anywhere nearby. Barn Owls, as noted under

GREAT HORNED OWL TALONS

that species, do inhabit the same immediate areas with the Great Horned Owl, partly because they have different food preferences.

There is a certain caution one should use in reading about owls which is appropriate at this point. If you read a book which lists all of the foods eaten by Great Horned Owls, the impression is likely to be that this owl eats as variedly as a Screech Owl. It is true that all of these things *can* be food for this owl and since it is more powerful, larger birds such as ducks, grouse, pheasant and shore birds, along with larger mammals like skunks, woodchucks and raccoons, will at times be found in the diet. The qualification is not that these facts are wrong, but that they conceal the truth that this owl has distinct preferences and where possible eats what it likes best. East or West the Horned Owl prefers cottontail rabbits above other kinds of prey. In the foothills of the Sierra Nevada, in California, studies of a number of these owls showed that up to 61% of the diet was the cottontail. In the West, wood rats, which are not entirely nocturnal and so can be hunted late in the day and at dusk, are the second most popular food. While gophers lead the rodents in numbers in many areas, they are a minor part of the food fare, as are snakes. Though there is this specialization, the preferred food will not be the same everywhere. In an area in Nevada, for example, more than half the food consisted of meadow mice. Clearly this owl balances preference with the abundance of major prey items, and thus serves the top-predator role as previously mentioned. To take another example, this time from Oklahoma, 118 lots of Horned Owl pellets were studied with the following percentages: cottontails 25%; pocket mice 18%; kangaroo rats 12%; grasshopper mice 10%. As opposed to these items only 4.7% of the food came from birds (Schemnitz 1962). All of the food lists indicate that any birds taken by Horned Owls will be large ones, such as domestic chickens, or other large birds like jays, woodpeckers, and other species of owls. Of songbirds almost nothing is heard in serious analyses of Horned Owl prey, which is not altogether a matter of size since insects are readily and often eaten, although they do not make up much of the bulk of the large owl's food.

The density of Horned Owls in any given amount of space is variable and differs between the nesting season and the remainder of the year. In a Wisconsin study over a large area, it appeared that two to five square miles were required for each pair, with a minimum distance between breeding pairs of a mile and a quarter, which was the territory defended, while they actually lived farther apart and had a more extensive feeding range. Another curious fact which came from the same study was the observation that not all of these owls pair up each year; as many as six pairs out of twenty were found to be non-breeding, the assumption being that these were yearlings. In a large tract in the California foothills it was determined that the density was much greater, for at least one Horned Owl lived in every hundred acres, which means that one could stand at almost any point and likely locate one of these owls (Fitch 1947). The actual hunting there was not at random and the birds often limited hunting to a few acres, night after night, and its targets were usually outcroppings of granite rock where the passages and crevices are runs for rodents and cottontail rabbits.

In the West, Horned Owls will inhabit many areas where the trees are scattered, either mixes of oak and Digger pine or pinyon-juniper country, but also they live up to 7000 feet and are not uncommon to 9000 or even 10,000 feet in well-forested mountains. Horned Owls also inhabit rugged lavabeds where there are few trees, and deserts where there are no trees, but which have cliffs and crevices for nesting protected by shade; and there are some which are beachcombers in the West. In the East the favored habitats are dense woods, the deeper the better if there is a choice, or the larger woodlots in farming country, where they will try to nest in the very center, usually in some abandoned Red-tailed Hawk nest high in a tree.

The eastern Horned Owl is just about the first bird of the season to nest in the central and northeastern part of the country (with the possible exception of a few Red Crossbills), some laying the two eggs which make up the standard clutch by the end of January. February is the normal month for incubation in the North, although they may begin as early as December in Florida. Because of the earliness of the season, subfreezing temperatures and even subzero readings are common, but these owls need this early start for their slow maturing young, and the female sits tightly in her wintry home. Both eggs and young are subject to predation by raccoons and in the West by Golden Eagles.

After the young have been raised, the adults return again to their solitary habits and it isn't until the fall and winter that hooting is heard once more. The deep, resonant call, a *hoo, hoohoo, hoo, hoo,* of the Horned Owl is probably the most familiar of all bird songs. It is associated with harvest moons and the chilling frosts of autumn and as the year grows colder and December turns to January, hooting increases as males and females speak to one another, the female in a shorter and higher sequence of notes with a less regular cadence. There is a comforting "all is well" quality about this major call as it comes from a clump of woods, either remote or near a farm, but the Horned Owl can make other sounds which are nothing but disturbing. The female has a catlike or hawklike screech or squawk, while the young have a downright scream which has chilled the spine of many a camper sleeping alone in the woods.

Since the distribution of this owl is so great, it has diverged into a number of subspecies, some of which are quite distinct in color. The Arctic Horned Owl is very light in both ground color and markings, while the dusky horned owl of the central California coastal forests, and northward, is quite dark, which emphasizes the white, triangular patch at its throat. The subspecies of the southwestern deserts (see western great horned owl on front cover) is again palely marked to blend with the sands. Wherever Great Horned Owls are found they tend to be resident birds, doing only a little local wandering. It is not hard to locate one of the birds for observation. When the sound of its voice has indicated a general area, wander around its outskirts a little after sundown. Quite possibly you will then see the owl flying out from its perch, or if you come upon it suddenly, the bird will likely fly slowly to another perch some distance away. Since the bird is larger than a Red-tailed Hawk and has prominent and erect ear tufts, plus a white throat, it will be easy to separate this species from any other owl. The Long-eared Owl does have tufts on its head, but these are closer together and that bird entirely lacks the broad-shouldered majesty of the Great Horned Owl. How shy the bird will be depends on where you are. Don Phillips says (in *litt.*) that those in Pennsylvania are very shy, probably because that state offered a bounty for their scalps until recently. In northern California, they will first let one know that they are not afraid and then retire to a distance, but with aloof dignity.

Don Phillips ©

SNOWY OWL *(Nyctea scandiaca)*

Specifics: Length: 20 to 28". Wingspread: 54 to 67". Weight: 3 to 6 lbs.

Range: Alaska, Canada and N. border states in winter, plus strays south (see N. A. distribution map 6, p. 23). Also Arctic Europe and Asia with irruptions south.

One would expect this very large white bird, whose home is in the North and the Arctic, to be a rare sight even to travelers, but by good fortune many bird watchers in the United States have had at least occasional glimpses of a Snowy Owl and at times, in a few places, these birds are seen in numbers. If an acquaintance claims that he has seen a Snowy Owl, the first thing to check is whether or not he knows the Barn Owl. Not that they look much alike, but in the dusk light underside of the Barn Owl may fool a novice. It has the unmistakable "monkey-face" and a body which is rather small for the size of its large head. The Snowy Owl is much larger, similar to the Great Horned Owl in weight and body size, while exceeding it in wingspan; but for all this bigness, its head is comparatively small and the eyes are set high on the "hornless" head, giving it a low-browed look. Some male Snowy Owls appear to be almost completely white, although most of them will carry brownish-black spotting or barring on the back and wings. Females and juveniles invariably show dark markings and barring, and always have more dense markings than adult males.

The high Arctic is the true home of these great white owls and they nest even to the farthest reaches: Point Barrow in Alaska is the northernmost point of land there, but on the eastern side of the conti-nent, land goes much farther north and nests have been found on Ellesmere Island, off the northern tip of Greenland at 80° and at Perryland (tip of Greenland) at 82° and 48 minutes north (Watson 1957).   On the Alaskan side the birds seem to be more or less resident, but elsewhere Snowy Owls migrate to the southern provinces of Canada for the winter season, not because the cold bothers them but because of lack of prey in the Arctic wasteland. The Snowy Owl is not a forest hunter, but prefers the open tundra or even salt marshes and sandy beaches, and depends on its keen, long-distance eyesight for spotting prey and also for spotting human beings of whom it is quite

SNOWY OWL SHOWING BARRING ON BACK AND WINGS   (*Photo by Don & Esther Phillips*)

shy. Usually it will keep a safe gunshot-distance between itself and observer, but in nesting season these owls will attack a man vigorously, particularly when there are growing young in the nest and as the oldest of these have begun to wander away from this center.

Accounts of this bird's nesting in Alaska [(Murie 1929) see also (Sutton and Parmelee 1956)] may be taken as typical for all areas, although the dates may vary for the more southern parts of its breeding range, which include northeastern Manitoba and the northern rim of Quebec. At the mouth of the Yukon in Alaska, numerous pairs of Snowy Owls select breeding sites on the bare ground, but usually on a slight rise or the mounds which are the result of frost heaves which provide a view of the surrounding terrain. A few nest on exposed ground in the tidal flats and some have even been found nesting on top of granite boulders. Most of the time the nest will be a slight scrape, some three or four inches deep and perhaps a foot across, made by removing lichen and mosses. The first eggs are laid about the 20th of May, which may not yet be a period of good weather, but the female will devote herself entirely to brooding the eggs while the male stands guard and hunts to bring in food for the pair. Eggs are laid perhaps every other day, with an average of eight eggs per clutch in this area. There can be as few as five or as many as ten eggs, giving this owl a potential for large increases in population for those years when lemmings or other prey are swarming. It will be remembered that the Great Horned Owl, by way of comparison, raises less than two young per pair each year.

Incubation takes from 32 to 37 days and, since the mother owl has been brooding from the time the first egg was laid, that first one will be hatched and the chick well-developed before its youngest sibling pecks through its shell. Because of this overlapping the mother has some difficulty in protecting all of her offspring. When the mother bird is off the nest during minutes or hours which may be bitterly cold, the newly hatched chicks, still in the early downy stage, will crawl under their older and warmer siblings that have heavier gray down. At times some will wander away from the "nest." Not that there are many predators brave enough to rob chicks from a Snowy Owl's nest, but there is an even greater danger from the weather which may be cold and rainy for days on end, or for the entire nesting period. The chicks that begin hatching at the end of June are white and for six to ten days have their eyes closed, after which their down becomes blue-grey in color; at the end of thirty days their faces only make a change to white, giving them the characteristic "dark jumpsuit and goggles look." By the second week in July primary wing feathers have begun to appear on the older chicks and the worst hazards are over, but apparently only about half of the chicks which hatch live through until the following fall.

Arctic lemmings, which look like large meadow mice, except for having a short tail, are, along with other kinds of mice, the primary food of these owls. The lemmings have peak years when they swarm over the tundra in almost limitless abundance, but those years are then followed by lesser populations and sometimes they are even scarce. Arctic hares are also a staple in the Snowy Owl diet, as are birds. It is during the nesting period that these owls destroy the greatest number of birds, both large and small. Lemmings may be primary but when there are as many as ten young mouths to feed everything available must be used. If the nest is near the coast, various kinds of shore birds are taken and larger birds such as ducks and even goslings may fall victims. Ptarmigan and other grouse are taken in winter, along with gulls, grebes and other water birds; even small birds, such as Snow Buntings and longspurs, are caught on the wing. Among fellow owls, the Short-eared, because it inhabits open places, most often falls victim to this greater predator. However, it is the teeming rodent populations which more often attract the keen eyes of Snowy Owls.

Visiting Snowy Owls seem to be rather silent birds, but perhaps that is because they are seldom seen during their courting season. When they do call, the voice is a hoarse one, the notes are low and the call is spoken of either as "booming" or as a hollow growl which transcribes: *whowh, whowh, whowh, hah, hah*. The booming call is given more often by males and is used for both courting and for threatening intruders into the male territory, and in either case its use is confined to the breeding season. A low cackling call of great variability is given between the sexes to indicate something like "hello," and both sexes when agitated will utter a *kre, kre, kre, kre, kre*, or an intensely shrill whistle. Away from their nests wariness toward man seems to prevail, in part because this owl hunts during the long Arctic daylight and can be seen from a distance. It has not the protection of darkness and forests which surround the Great Horned Owl in its home. In hunting, which takes place in all weathers and at all hours, the Snowy Owl flies close above its prey, then sinks its talons down into the animal's vitals. If the animal is large, as in the case of an Arctic hare (which will weigh twice as much as the bird), the owl will pump its wings to act as a brake and slow the contest to a halt.

It was mentioned at the beginning that many people have seen this northern owl in various parts of the U. S. A few of the Snowy Owls spend the winter in northern Greenland or Alaska, but most of them retreat southward, with the greatest number staying in southern Canada. Some, however, come into New England and even as far as New Jersey and Pennsylvania. Strays make it much farther with records from Bermuda, and in the West from southern California and Wichita Falls, Texas (Gross 1947) (Hanson 1971). In some years there are notable invasions by masses of Snowy Owls, at which time they can be seen along our northern border. Unfortunately great numbers of these have been killed in the past, either as enemies of game, or simply to mount for the mantlepiece. One of the most famous of these invations took place in the winter of 1926-27, particularly covering Michigan and Maine. Some 5000 owls were said to have been shot that winter. The winter of 1945-46 was another such period, as was 1966-67 in the Northwest. As an example of winter records in the U. S., 1976-77 may be cited. There were fewer than normal reports from the Northeast, but a normal number of sightings from the northern Great Plains, while Iowa had the greatest invasion of "Snowies" in fifty years. Elsewhere these owls were seen in southwestern Pennsylvania, southern Virginia, Shreveport, Louisiana, Oklahoma City, and at twelve different localities in Kansas. There were also occasional sightings in Colorado, Montana and Washington states ("Winter Season" 1977).

In California there have been scattered sightings of these owls through the years, but these were based on sheer luck of the observer. More recently the best place to go, if one wants to plan on seeing a Snowy Owl in this state, is along the northern coast in Humboldt County. These owls apparently make their way down the coastline from Alaska with some regularity, a number having been seen in 1967 and since. In 1977 one appeared on the mud-flats of Humboldt Bay near Arcata on November 24. In other years they have been seen in that area from December to March, hunting the flats and sand dunes there.

Don Phillips ©

HAWK OWL *(Surnia ulula)*

Specifics: Length: 14 to 17". Wingspread: 31 to 35". Weight: 9 to 14 ozs.

Range: Alaska & Canada, except far North; similar area in Europe & Asia (see N. A. distribution map 7, p. 24).

The first sight of a Hawk Owl will likely come as a surprise, unless one has made a trip to Canada with that observation as one of the goals, because it is a rare owl within the U. S., not common in Canada and its appearance and habits are so little like other owls. Once found, the Hawk Owl is easy enough to watch since all of its activity belongs to the daylight hours, as indicated by its old common name of "day owl." Roland C. Clement described the habits of this owl near Indian Lake, Labrador (in Todd 1963, p. 446) as it responded to his imitation of jay calls.

Then it dropped from its high perch, swooped low over me, and bounded upward to another spruce top. This was characteristic behavior because the Hawk Owl always plummets downward upon taking off, and, after wheeling through the woods, rises abruptly to a new lookout. Few birds are more dashing in the woods than this diurnal owl. Its long wings beat through deep arcs, or they are held stiffly as the bird manoeuvers through the trees at breathtaking speed.

The versatile Hawk Owl can not only make its way through brush like a Sharp-shinned Hawk, but it can also hover over open places like the American Kestrel (sparrow hawk). Returning to perch, it will sit and flick its long tail, again like the American Kestrel. It is a medium-sized owl, smaller than a Barn Owl, and about the size of a Cooper's Hawk, with head and eyes that are small and falcon-shaped—except for the presence of facial discs which are buffy-white set off by black around eyes and border. The hawk simulation is continued with a lean body and tight plumage for an owl; its flight is not so silent either. A capping similarity is that the voice of this owl is a hawklike scream, which has been transcribed as *ku—wee*, or *que-reek*. At other times the screech will be a *rike, rike, rike* or a more chattering *kikikikikiki*. Again it may be a whistled call something like an American Kestrel, and when flying a *whir-u, whir-u*.

Hawk Owls inhabit the boreal region of Canada and Alaska, and similar regions across Siberia and northern Europe. The subspecies in the latter regions is much lighter in color than in the North American specimens. This owl does not go into the far north as the Snowy Owl does. It likes at least a few trees nearby even when hunting over open territory. It prefers muskeg bogs within forests, burnt over, or scrubland, and slow streams that spill over to become marshes. The Hawk Owl will sit on a dead treetop and survey the open ground or bog below for signs of lemmings, mice, squirrels, a few songbirds and the like, which, along with insects, are its principal summer foods. In winter they make a specialty of catching grouse and snowshoe hares, but they seldom eat small birds in any season.

Don Phillips found the Hawk Owl illustrated in this book (Color Plate VII, p. 119) in the Baskalong Reservoir area of Quebec, Canada, where it was presiding over a muskeg, thick with blackflies and other insects. The bogs in the area were covered with sphagnum moss and surrounded by a dense growth of trees, which made passage difficult. This owl was clothed in the neat, chocolate-brown plumage of its kind, spotted white on the back and with light undersides broadly barred on both breast and belly. True to its reputation, the bird ignored the intruder (Phillips) as he sloshed around in his hip-waders. This species of owl seems to have no fear of man whatsoever, even though it must hunt and spend the day in open view. Probably, because its hunting grounds are remote and difficult of access, it has not, generally, studied enough men to develop a reasonable fear of them. At one point during the two-hour watch this Hawk Owl swooped down to pick up either a mouse or a frog, then returned to the perch to eat it. These owls do not seem to be as greedy in their feeding habits as most owls are, and instead of swallowing food whole they tear it to shreds as they eat, again much like a hawk. The flight is rapid and direct to the prey which is snatched, then carried in the talons during a continuing flight near the ground until the owl finally shoots up to the perch at a sharp angle.

While the Hawk Owl is not afraid of man, neither is it friendly to him during the nesting season and there are several accounts of the male owl drawing blood from birders who were climbing a tree toward the nest. These owls are said to build crude nests of their own with a few sticks gathered together, usually where a limb has broken off and rotted down; they will also use an abandoned woodpecker cavity with no nesting material. From three to seven or eight white eggs are laid, with the middle number being the most common, beginning in April and continuing through May. The earlier dates for laying relate to the south of the breeding range and nesting becomes progressively later in higher latitudes. For feeding the young, grasshoppers and other insects are an important part of the diet, along with the abundant mice and various other small mammals. The chicks seem to be everlastingly hungry and discontented in the nest, and they keep up a continuous hissing and whistling which can be heard on the ground, thus giving away the position of the nest. Apparently the parents are fully capable of protecting the young from weasels, martins or other predators as the only true enemy of Hawk Owls is that lord of all forests, the Great Horned Owl, which will take both adults and young of this species.

For those who would like to see this diurnal owl without taking a trip into the wilds of Canada or Alaska, there are possibilities within

(Hawk Owl continued on page 121)

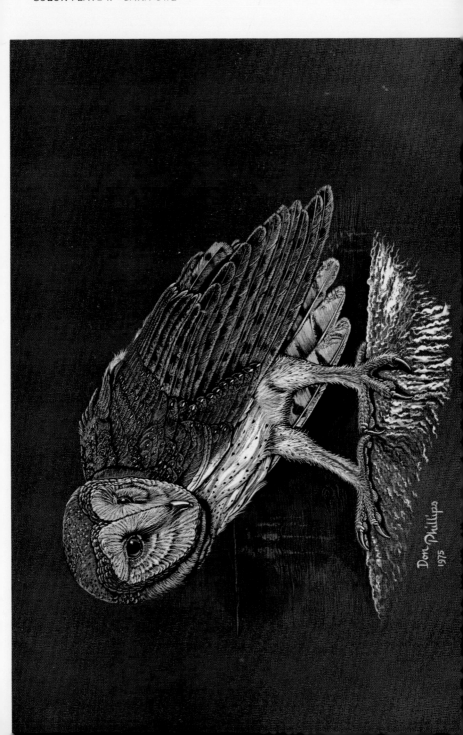

Don Phillips
Sept. 17-18, 1975

the U. S. In winter it is found in the northern parts of Washington, Idaho and Montana, with the area around the northern end of Flathead Lake in Montana being a particularly good spot for sightings. Both the Dakotas and Nebraska have had sightings commonly, as have the areas around the Great Lakes and the northeastern states, particularly Maine. To find these birds during the breeding season the nearest point for easterners would be New Brunswick and for those of the West, northern British Columbia or central Alberta.

It is quite a step from this owl which in so many ways has departed from the norms of other owls, to the likewise diurnal gnome of an owl which has overemphasized all owl characteristics, possibly to compensate for his small size: the Pygmy Owl.

PYGMY OWL *(Glaucidium gnoma)*

Specifics: Length: 6 to 7.5". Wingspread: 14.5 to 16". Weight: 2 to 3 ozs.

Range: Rockies to W. coast (see N. A. distribution map 8, p. 24); also higher mts. from Mexico to Honduras.

There are two closely related species of pygmy owls, the Ferruginous which follows, and this one. The Pygmy Owl is a very small, sparrow-sized, but chunky owl which seldom weighs over two and a half ounces. It has a completely fierce disposition which belies its minute size for an owl, and it is a terror among songbirds, woodpeckers, and even quail. Although it is common in many parts of the West, most people never see this owl: since, when it flies it darts through the bushes like any other small bird and is not recognized as an owl; on the other hand, when it is perched on some high pine limb, it looks very much like a cone that might belong in that place and thus again passes unnoticed.

One does have frequent chances to see this owl, however, because it is largely diurnal, feeding in early morning and late afternoon; it does not even hide in a cavity during midday, but rather assumes a convenient perch and nods away the noontide. The way it will most often be noticed is by the throng of songbirds noisily attacking it, for mobbing scenes are a daily occurrence. Once spotted, both this species and the Ferruginous Owl have a perfect recognition mark—on the back of their necks are a pair of black, false eyespots, with prominent white margins. These marks, which undoubtedly have some value in protecting these birds against attack from behind, are unique, and have given them a Mexican nickname that translates "Four-Eyes."

Pygmy Owls inhabit woodlands and mountain forests of the West, breeding from near sea level on the coast to 10,000 feet in the Colorado Rockies. The other small owl which occupies much of this same territory is the Saw-whet Owl, but the latter is nocturnal, lacks the "four eyes" and has a proportionately larger squarish head and a short tail. The Pygmy, by contrast, has a small head with scarcely developed facial discs and a long, white-barred tail which it holds at an angle, or flicks to express excitement. Both species have light underparts with vertical streaks, but in the Pygmy these are sharply defined and dark brown or nearly black. About its crown the Pygmy Owl displays numerous small, round, white or buffy dots, in contrast to the streaks of a Saw-whet.

Quite by chance a Pygmy Owl became a personable friend of mine. This recent friendship began while my wife and I were returning from an unsuccessful quest for sight of a Great Gray Owl in Yosemite. The truck was humming along a downhill stretch outside the park when I was suddenly struck a smart blow on the forehead and since my window was nearly closed I started with alarm, but the next moment found a groggy Pygmy in my lap and an opportunity to study this owl at close quarters. "Halfdome," as he was promptly named, had a capacity for adjusting to surprising circumstances. After reviving and passing through a beak and talon phase, he quickly decided that we were neither food nor foe and might even be friends.

Halfdome was exceptionally alert in responding to every change in his surroundings, checking out each new sound or sight. If several people were talking together, he was a perfect listener, shifting his full attention to each speaker in turn. While all owls use beak-snapping as a defense or warning signal, this fellow quickly learned that snapping could be used equally well to call for food, or just for the attention he enjoyed. This Pygmy, unlike most larger owls, never swallowed food whole; whether mouse, salamander or bird, he carefully picked it a bite at a time. Since his residence here coincided with a massive Starling invasion, neighboring farmers supplied these birds, which Halfdome would hang casually by one talon, behind his perch. An hour or so later he might remove a few feathers, then wait longer until the ritual peck at the base of the bird's skull began his feast. While eating at a slow pace, the Pygmy kept the feathered carcass up under him so that the feathers of both predator and prey were as one, largely concealing the slow business of consumption.

One morning Halfdome's improvised cage was set outside in the November sun, but in no time at all small birds discovered his presence in *their* garden. A mobbing attack was led by a pair of Plain Titmice with several Golden-crowned Sparrows circling the cage; a few feet back, eight Oregon Juncos scolded from low tree branches; from a low bush on the other side, a Lesser Goldfinch and a pair of Ruby-crowned Kinglets contributed, minutely, to the din; and a Bewick's Wren hopped right out in front of the cage. The second line of this chorus came from an entire family of Western Bluebirds which were joined in a more distant tree by two Robins. Halfdome returned the mobbing birds' fury in kind with beak-snapping and a flexing of talons on the cage roof.

This Pygmy Owl's nature was to be unafraid in a basic sense and never to panic. My wife and I had measured his 6.2 inches of power and then wanted to know his weight; for that he was shut up in a shoebox of known heft. Even in that strait he submitted calmly, without wing-flutterings or struggle, while we learned that, full fed, he weighed a little over two and a half ounces. Then alas, since he was as vigorous as wise, it seemed unfair to confine so perfect a wild creature, thus the Sierran subspecies was given flight to join Pygmy Owls of our darker coastal race.

As a daytime hunter, the Pygmy Owl takes a number of small mammals, among which chipmunks are notable—in New Mexico its fondness is for the rock chipmunk (J. S. Ligon 1961). Mice are also important as are insects which can be caught on the wing. Young chicks first learn to feed on such insects and then graduate to bite size morsels, which they are fed by the parent owls. While on family matters, the mating call of Pygmy Owls somewhat resembles the cooing of doves, with those notes followed by a *cuk, cuk, cuk*. The major call is an evenly spaced, mellow whistle, *to, to, to, to*, often ending with a *took* or *si-poolk*. Near the nest the female, which will lay three or four eggs in an old woodpecker hole, gives a soft twitter in response to the food-bringing male, but he does not come to the nest, nor take any part in feeding the young.

When attacking other birds in the air the Pygmy Owl dives with folded wings and a falcon-like spirit, seizing birds as large as full grown woodpeckers. One such assault, on a Nuttall's Woodpecker in California, is typical. The Pygmy struck its prey, which was at least as heavy as the attacker, and dug in its needle sharp talons as both birds fell to the ground. There the owl dispatched the woodpecker with a blow of its hooked beak (Brock 1958). It is a curious, though logical fact that the flight sounds of this little owl are not muffled as they are in most other owls, and can be heard if one is standing close enough.

Among their own kind these owls keep a regulated distance of a mile between pairs in places where the population is dense, and they hunt within that territory. Often, however, they are widely scattered and can easily live in privacy. How great their ambition may be is illustrated in the account of an attack on a grown quail by a Pygmy Owl which weighed 1.75 ounces; the victim was twice the weight and size of the owl. Not all attacks are successful and at times snakes or weasels will turn tables and kill the attacking owl, but that possibility does not daunt it. There are accounts of jays actually killing Pygmy Owls during mobbings, and the Spotted Owl will make a meal of this midget relative on occasion. Most of these little owls are able to maintain a carefree existence despite these perils. They have one habit which rather signals this attitude: a number of large owls will take to the water to pick up fish and some bathe at times, but the Pygmy Owl thoroughly enjoys a noonday bath and any number have been seen, even in gardens, bathing away as happily as any Brown Towhee in a concrete birdbath. In nature they do the same in pools and springs, keeping themselves perky and feather-bright.

FERRUGINOUS OWL *(Glaucidium brasilianum)*

Specifics: Length: 6 to 7". Wingspread: 14.5 to 16". Weight: 2 to 3 ozs.

Range: border area of Arizona, New Mexico, Texas, S. to tip of South America (see N. A. distribution map 9, p. 25).

The proper common name of this species is now simply, Ferruginous Owl, meaning the rusty one, but that name doesn't indicate to the general reader the important fact that this is also a pygmy owl and a companion species to the Pygmy Owl of the West. The genus *Glaucidium* contains a dozen species well distributed around the world: India, Southeast Asia, Africa, the New World, and one Eurasian Pygmy Owl whose realm extends from Norway and France to China. The latter species is a little larger than our two and, for the casual observer, the chief distinction is that the streakings on its belly and the ground color of the tail are olive-brown. In other words, the Eurasian species and the two which inhabit the U. S. have diverged very little from one another.

Probably the most distinctive thing about the Ferruginous Owl is its distribution, which includes the Strait of Magellan, Chile, Brazil, Guiana, Central America, both coasts of Mexico, and the southwestern U. S. border states.   In Texas it is found from Brownsville upriver to Hildalgo County, while in Arizona it inhabits the desert region of the south-central and southwestern sections; Ligon (Ligon, J. S. 1961) does not even list this species for New Mexico, so it is only a presumption there along the Mexican border.

Ferruginous Owls have the black, false eyespots on the back of their neck, just as Pygmy Owls do, but the tail differs from that species.   In the Ferruginous Owl of Arizona, the tail is always rusty-colored with seven or eight *brown* bars crossing it (the Pygmy has narrow white bars and fewer of them).   Also of value in distinguishing the two is the fact that the Ferruginous has streaks on top of the head while these are spots on the Pygmy Owl.   While these points are slight, one can rely on distribution to separate the two species.   The Ferruginous Owl inhabits mesquite thickets, thorn scrub and thorn forests—in Arizona it is mostly in the saguaro cactus desert or mesquite thickets; the Pygmy Owl does not descend to elevations this low.   Within the saguaro cactus habitat there is another small owl, the Elf Owl, which also lives in cavities carved out of the cactus by woodpeckers and flickers.   The latter owl is smaller and its tail is very much shorter, not extending beyond the wings when at rest.   The Elf Owl is also nocturnal, while the Ferruginous Owl is largely diurnal, although it calls both by day and night.

The alert reader will note that Don Phillips has placed both the Ferruginous and Pygmy owls on the same color plate, a conjunction not likely to be found in nature. Sketches for the Ferruginous Owl were made one hot day in Mexico along the Rio Sabina, north of Ciudad Victoria, Tamaulipas.   Phillips had been collecting insects in the area, and with his wife was resting in the shade of some welcome cypress trees when a commotion in a nearby tangled thicket attracted their attention.   On approaching the center of the din, they found a tumult of small birds, led by a flock of Green Jays, trying to reach a little Ferruginous Owl concealed in acacia and mesquite.   The owl sat calmly in his thorn-protected bower, and with the approach of human intruders the jays backed off for a time while the owl resumed his nap. After thinking through the situation further, the Green Jays returned to the attack with vigor and one almost reached the owl, which then made its way deeper into the thicket.

A curious thing about this little owl is that it will not fly or change its position at night, even if it is moonlit. Once a night-perch has been selected they stay there until the early morning hunting hours. Phillips, who imitates this owl well for calling purposes, gives the call as a rapidly repeated series of from ten to sixty loud but mellow *wuh's*. Others have referred to these as "chuffing" notes, and the birds will respond to them either by night or day, but the bird only comes up to the caller in daylight. Captain C. Bendire notes that it has a soft call, a *"chuck"* which can only be heard for a short distance.

The Ferruginous Owl was described from South America in the year 1800, but it was nearly three quarters of a century later that Bendire first located it within U. S. borders (Bendire 1892). In 1872 he took several of these owls in the mesquite thickets near Tucson, in January, which indicated to him that the owl was a resident species. At a later time he found nests and eggs in early May near Brownsville, Texas, in an old woodpecker hole. Eggs of the Ferruginous Owl differ from those of the Pygmy Owl in having much thicker shells which are rather coarsely granulated and they lack the pitting present in eggs of the latter species. It might be noted here that the Elf Owl, which also nests in holes in the saguaro cactus, has glossy eggs. There are other birds which would also like to nest in the few available holes, but the Ferruginous Owl has first choice and like its companion species preys on small birds, as well as reptiles and amphibians of the Lower Sonoran zone. Mice are again important, along with other small mammals, and insects probably are even more important to this species, which will forage somewhat like a flycatcher in the first fifteen feet or so above the desert surface.

Despite the implications of rusty tones in the name, the owl has both a gray-brown and a red form, with those from Arizona being a decidedly pale gray, except for the tail which is rusty-colored. Ferruginous Owls in lower Texas are the proper rusty-brown which justifies the name.

DoN Phillips ©

ELF OWL *(Microthene whitneyi)*

Specifics: Length: 5 to 6". Wingspread: 14 to 15". Weight: 1 to 1.7 ozs.*

Range: S. Arizona to central Mexico (see N. A. distribution map 10, p. 25).

The Elf Owl is as different from the Pygmy Owl as night from day, and in fact, the Elf Owl is a night feeder while the Pygmy Owl is diurnal. But the greatest difference is that the Elf Owl is so delicate that it can be knocked out of the air by a robin, while the Pygmy Owl is, as mentioned earlier, ferocious enough to tackle a quail twice its own size. When an Elf Owl is attacked by a robin or other small- to medium-sized bird, the aggression is unwarranted since the Elf Owl eats nothing larger than a scorpion, never takes birds of any kind, and is almost entirely insectivorous, if we include other arthropods in that category. Like the Pygmy Owl, the Elf Owl can also be said to be sparrow-sized, but it will have to be a small sparrow—perhaps a Rufous-crowned with a little more pad-

*(J. D. Ligon 1968, p. 27)

ding is about the right size for comparison. It will weigh in at from an ounce to nearly an ounce and three quarters, while the Pygmy Owl will go on up to two and a half or three ounces, making a sort of feather-weight vs. bantamweight division.

Elf Owls have a grayish-brown upperside which is spotted with buff, while the underparts are white, softly and indefinitely marked with brown (no definite streaks or bars). Eyebrows are notably pen-ciled in white and since the range of this species overlaps that of the Ferruginous Owl, the distinctions between the two should be kept in mind. The Elf Owl has no black false-eye patches on the back of its neck, and has a very short tail (the Ferruginous is long-tailed). Some of the voice-language of the Elf Owl was covered in Chapter 4, pp. 54 + 57. Its characteristic call is a kind of high-pitched chatter: *whi-whi-whi-whi-whi*, or *chewk-chewk-chewk* etc., or as others hear that one—*tyew-tyew*, etc. These notes are delivered rapidly and sometimes the call has a puppylike yip in the middle.

Elf Owls are always thought of as denizens of saguaro cactus, which indeed they often are. These great treelike plants provide perfect insulation for the owls during torrid desert days. Because of their small surface area, Elf Owls have difficulty in regulating their temperature; therefore, the insulation provided in the depths of a cavity within the giant cactus is most useful during the breeding season, which is in the hottest part of the year, and the same protection is also given during daytime roosting in the holes. The cavity furthermore provides them with water economy, just like the burrows used by small mammals on the desert, and preservation of water content is vital in their arid environ-ment. If, however, the Elf Owls are at higher elevations they nest in holes in sycamore or pine trees. For a complete biology of the Elf Owl see: (Ligion, J. D. 1968, 1969).

This is another species of owl which was long known south of the border, but had to wait for discovery on the northern side. In 1861 John Cooper found the Elf Owl near Ft. Mojave, on the Arizona side of the Colorado River, but it was not until 1904 that it was also found on the opposite bank and added to the California fauna. A decade later Dr. Grinnell of the University of California again found the bird on this side, in a three-branched saguaro cactus which was eighteen feet tall and two feet in diameter. The Elf Owl's cavity was twelve feet up and just a foot lower than that, on the opposite side, an American Kestrel had a nest with five eggs in a second hole. This proclivity for apartment dwelling is typical of the tiny owl. In Arizona Joe Marshall, Jr. reports Elf Owls and Acorn Woodpeckers using the same cavity in shifts, the owl by day and the woodpecker at night.

The summer range of the migratory Elf Owl includes a desert slice of southeastern California, and they are abundant in southern Arizona below the heavy pine forest elevation, also not uncommon in southwestern New Mexico. Their territory is discontinuous, beginning again in the Big Bend area of Texas in summer; farther down the river, in Hidalgo County the Elf Owl is becoming a common resident again, particularly in Benson State Park. The appearance of Elf Owls along and north of the Mexican boundary in the West is entirely seasonal, since the insects on which the owls feed become inactive or scarce in winter, at which time Elf Owls make a regular winter migration to southwestern Mexico. Before undertaking this journey the owls gather together in flocks and in October begin to make their way south to the Rio Balsas Basin where the climate is tropical, though arid. In parts of this area there are no trees or large cacti for holing up, but the warm nights abound with insects for owls. Some of these owls return to their breeding grounds in Arizona at the end of February and by mid-March most of the Elves are again present.

All that a pair needs for nesting is some kind of hole, provided by an Acorn, Gila, or Arizona woodpecker in sycamores or pines; and by the Gilded Flicker in the giant cacti. The male first lays claim to one of these cavities and the foraging ground around it, and then announces his presence to all. While he doesn't mind other birds as close neighbors, other Elf Owls are not allowed during the nesting season, so the male pipes its song to warn away other Elf males and entice a mate to join him in the cavity. When a female shows interest he sings her all the way to the cavity opening and then descends ahead and sings on a more personal note from the bottom of his cavity. If she enters he then leaves and stands guard outside. Once settled, she lays from two to four eggs and gives full attention to incubation while the male devotes himself to feeding her, and then the chicks.

Food for both young and adults consists of arthropods, up to the size of scorpions, with flying moths and beetles being picked up while foraging in low runs near the ground, or the Elf Owl may fly into the leaves of oaks in mountain areas and stir up a crowd of small insects there; on the desert, cactus blooms are a similar focus for insect food. Joe Marshall, Jr. describes some of the comic antics of this minute predator while trying to eat a hawk moth.

> The prey is transferred from one foot to the bill, then to the other foot and so on, the bird meanwhile standing high on its long legs, as if to avoid mussing its plumage; the ankles are bent together to give it a comical knock-kneed appearance. After several minutes of handling a large hawk moth, one Elf Owl had accomplished nothing more than biting the head and attempting to take off the wings. (Marshall 1957, p. 78)

There is no haste in gathering food when one's body weighs little more than an ounce, since a few insects will do; and why not enjoy the consideration and leisure that this fact allows. All of this insect-feeding is done at dusk or afterwards through the night. During the incubation period, which lasts 24 days, the female also has a chance to forage for herself and stretch a bit at dusk, but soon returns to her duty where she is concealed from the world. After the chicks have hatched, the male continues to feed her and the young until the demands have grown too large for one bird to supply, then the female joins her mate foraging in order to feed the nestlings which remain in the cavity for from 28 to 33 days.

This very small predator, which is obviously on a bypath in the evolution of owls, has by-passed as well all of their ferocious ways. As might be expected, the Elf Owl has no near relatives whatsoever and remains the solitary species of its genus. Those who stand apart from the crowd's direction often do so alone.

Don Phillips ©

BURROWING OWL *(Athene* cunicularia)*
(until 1976 in genus *Speotyto*)

Specifics: Length: 8.5 to 11". Wingspread: 22 to 24". Weight: 4.5 to 8 ozs.

Range: western half of U. S., down through South America; C. & S. Florida & West Indies (see N. A. distribution map 11, p. 26).

While the Elf Owl has found one way to be different, the Burrowing Owl has added two more characteristics which set it apart from other owls. Most medium and large owls, and not a few smaller ones, are solitary by nature. Barn Owls do of course roost together in wintertime and, as we have seen, the Elf Owls collect together for a short period before beginning their southward migration; but as a group, owls are solitary birds with few flocking instincts—except for this species. Burrowing

*Thirty-third Supplement to A.O.U. Check-list. Oct. 1976. *Auk* 93:875-879 (see p. 877). The statement is: *"Speotyto* is merged in the genus *Athene,* but is retained as a subgenus."

Owls do like to live together with others of their kind in colonies, at any place where the food supply is abundant. When prairie dog communes dotted the open West in times past, communes of Burrowing Owls lived right alongside of them. An even greater divergence from standard owlness is their ground dwelling habit; they feed on top of the ground and uniquely they find or dig out nests underground. In addition, they have no need for woods to haunt, or even of trees from which to hunt—a fencepost will do for a hunting perch and if even that is unavailable this owl can get along perfectly with only the mound at the entrance to its burrow for an observation point.

There is no difficulty identifying this middling-sized owl with its very long, bare, knock-kneed legs. When seen, the Burrowing Owl does not attempt to conceal itself except to remain half-in and half-out of its hole. The male will stand guard above ground during the nesting season, and year-round. The expression on the owl's quizzical face is always one of surprise mixed with disdain, and it keeps both eyes on the observer by twisting neck and head about to follow his movements until one fears that the head may become unscrewed and drop off. Finally, as it becomes more and more excited the small figure begins to bob up and down rapidly, a characteristic which has given it the name of "howdy owl" in Florida. The Burrowing Owl will be more readily recognized by these habits than by its physical characters: wings which are long for the bird's size, a short tail, upper parts which are brown, spotted and barred with buff, while the underparts reverse that pattern and are buff spotted with brown. The questioning look of this owl is the result of arching white eyebrow-streaks which are matched by a white ruff at the throat.

To see this owl commonly one has to live or travel in the West or in Florida. It ranges from the southwestern provinces of Canada, through western Nebraska and Kansas—to the western prairies of Minnesota during spring and summer. It may winter anyplace in the state of Texas, though distribution leans to the western part where it also breeds. In central and southern Florida, one may also see a subspecies, which is slightly smaller than its western counterpart. Since the Burrowing Owls tend to wander they have been recorded once in Massachusetts, in North Carolina and Alabama, and recently in Louisiana and at Jones Beach, New York ("Winter Season" 1977). The Burrowing Owl was formerly the single species in the genus *Speotyto*, but it has recently been combined with three Eurasian species in the genus *Athene*. The area covered by our Burrowing Owl is wide and includes all of South America except the Amazon Basin.

There are two principal requirements for this owl: a treeless plain which should be flat or only gently rolling, and burrows of some kind which can be used for nesting. A qualification should be added to the first requirement since the level ground should also not be cultivated, as plowing destroys the burrows and mounds. Naturally enough, most level ground has been used by farmers for cultivation so there are far fewer owls of this species than there used to be. However, they have learned to make use of some modern waste ground, like the level and cleared strips surrounding airports, the right-of-ways of railroads and highways and even unplowed ground along fence rows (Coulombe 1971) (Thomsen 1971) (Ligon, J. D. 1963). The burrows used to be provided by prairie dog dens over much of this owl's range, but the latter have been poisoned to extinction in most places. Nevertheless there are still the burrows of ground squirrels, badger dens, kangaroo rat tunnels, various kinds of culverts, or in Florida the burrows of the land tortoise and the armadillo.

Burrowing Owls apparently can't dig an entire den for themselves, but, by pecking away with their beaks and then scratching out the extra dirt with their feet, they are able to make great improvements on any hole that is already there. Such a burrow may be from four to ten feet long with an enlargement at the end and a variable depth. I recall one dug out by my father which was nine feet long with the nest end three feet below the ground surface. The entire tunnel and nest was covered with a layer of finely pulverized horse manure, which was still plentiful on farm land, and the result was much like spreading out a layer of peat moss. There were eleven eggs in that nest—the maximum but not unusual number. Because of the hazards, clutches are always large, with a minimum of five eggs. On the Palmetto prairies of southern Florida the water table is quite near the ground surface, so the depths of burrows are only fourteen to twenty inches and sometimes the terminal chamber is brought up above that level to prevent a torrential downpour from drowning out the nest.

Elevation is not a determining factor for Burrowing Owls, but it happens that most prairie lands are at lower levels than forested mountains. In California they inhabit valley floors in the Lower Sonoran zone, the islands off the coast at sea level, the bottom of Death Valley which is 200 feet below sea level, or the barren plateaus in the northeastern part of the state at elevations up to 5300 feet. In Colorado there is another step upward, providing breeding records to 9000 feet in suitable localities.

In the northern part of its range the Burrowing Owl seems to be somewhat migratory. It breeds in the Okanagan Region of Washington State and of British Columbia and on the prairies of Alberta and Saskatchewan, but definitely migrates southward from there in winter, at which time they also leave Minnesota and South Dakota. In most of the prairie sections of Montana, however, the birds are permanent residents. These owls can stand a great deal of cold by simply retreating underground during the worst weather and coming out to hunt on a fine day. In the Albuquerque area of New Mexico these owls migrate in late summer and only two or three birds of a large colony could be found in mid-winter (Martin 1973). In Arizona these owls seem to be permanent residents with only those in the northeast section becoming fall transients.

The month of the nesting season depends on the elevation of the owl's home. Since insects are important in the diet, they can't begin to nest before the onset of the bug season, which is April for the lowlands and progressively later as one goes upward. For high elevations in Colorado, it may be June or even July before nesting takes place. To make the colonial nesting establishment as harmonious as possible these ground owls often mate for life with only the females engaging in incubation of the eggs while the male stands guard near the burrow entrance and brings food to his mate morning and evening. At the least sign of danger the male will confront the intruder, by first addressing him directly and then after turning around he will make the same speech in the opposite direction. Scientists say that this puts him in a position to flee if necessary, but usually the owl will approach the predator with "chuck" calls and at times attack it with a startling scream—no mean feat if the intruder is a dog or a Great Horned Owl. The female may, during this encounter, keep her head just out of the burrow to check on the outcome and if there is the least doubt she will disappear below to protect the chicks. During the mating and nesting season the male and female keep up a constant exchange of mellow cooing notes which my father transcribed as *kook-ka—wah*, a melodious dialogue that floats over open fields just as darkness falls and which may also be heard at night. The business note of this owl is a cuckling *cack, cack, cack*, or *quick-quick-quick* which will become very emphatic if one approaches too close. A final warning may be exact mimicry, by the Burrowing Owl, of a rattlesnake's rattle, which must instinctively alarm many predators (Thomsen 1971).

On fine days the parent owls will bring the whole family of chicks out to sun and stand them in a line for airing, which is badly needed because in their underground burrow refuse collects around the young birds. Much of the food gathering by the adults is done on the ground where they scurry about with an odd gait that is sometimes like the jerky movements of cartoon figures. If they fly it is only for short bursts of no considerable distance and they hover before pouncing on their prey, if it is a small mammal. They do eat mice, but not to the same extent as many other owls. An analysis of food pellets made in Arizona indicated that scorpions led the list, followed by two families of ground beetles, then locusts, while pocket mice were fifth in importance. In both Florida and Colorado, crustaceans have been noted as being toward the top of food lists, while a Nevada count showed spadefoot toads and beetles, with no birds reported. Elsewhere, birds and particularly the nestlings of such species as Brewer's Blackbirds and Black Terns, have been found in the Burrowing Owl's burrows. At the entrance to one California burrow I noted a headless horned toad, a small frog and a scorpion—all to be used for a future dinner I presume. There is some evidence that Burrowing Owls may at times eat the young of prairie dogs, but that may be a matter of sheer chance since for the most part they seem to live in harmony with ground squirrel and prairie dog neighbors, and it is probable that the latter provide the owls a buffer against snakes. There is no end to the stories, but no facts, on what takes place when rattlesnakes and Burrowing Owls meet; if the snakes can get into the burrow they doubtless eat eggs and young, and skunks certainly rob Burrowing Owl nests. But that is why the female Burrowing Owl often lays nearly a dozen eggs in a clutch.

BARRED OWL *(Strix varia)*

Specifics: Length: 16 to 24". Wingspread: 38 to 50". Weight: 1 to 2.3 lbs.

Range: wooded parts east of Rocky Mts., recently westward in N. (see N. A. distribution map 12, p. 26); wooded parts of Mexican plateau to Oaxaca and Veracruz.

This large, hornless owl is easily distinguished by day since it is the only very large eastern owl with dark eyes, while at night the Barred Owl has a voice sufficiently distinctive to set it apart from any other species of owl. It is probably the noisiest and most talkative of the owls in its range, with the main call a hoot, but the hoot is easily distinguishable from the call of the Great Horned Owl. Its phrase consists of two sets of four *hoo's* ending with a downward break—notes which can readily be put into English to read: *Who cooks for you? Who cooks for you, all?* They have other calls of course, including a hoot that breaks off with a diminishing *Waahh-ah* that fades away, or a pleasant duet of the pair with one on a higher tone and twice as fast, and a number of weird chuckles, screams, and assorted haunted-house noises. Some of its calls resemble or overlap those of the eastern Screech Owl, but the deeper hoots will distinguish the voices of the two.

The name of this owl comes from the very distinctive horizontal barring of its feathers, including a puffy ruff around the throat and upper breast. Below that, on the underside, the Barred Owl has vertical brown streaking on a light background. The head is large and round, hornless, and the general appearance of the bird is chunky. Despite its large size, it has none of the fierceness of aspect which the even larger Great Horned Owl presents to the world, and this appearance reflects its less aggressive attitude—seldom will it attack a man even if he approaches its nest. Barred Owls are most likely to be found in deep forests or wooded swamps, or in Texas along river woodlands. In Florida, where it is the most abundant owl, the common name for it is the "swamp owl," which pretty much explains its habitat there. While they require deep woods rather than just a small patch of trees for a home base, in the East they do more hunting outside of woods than Great Horned Owls do, coming into farming fields and on occasion even into small towns.

Barred Owls have made a recent and rather unexpected expansion of their range along the U. S. - Canadian border, westward beyond Alberta and the mountains of eastern British Columbia which were always within the domain of this eastern owl. This westward extension of breeding birds first came to light in 1965 and since then there have been sightings along the border to the coast and up the inland passage as far as Cortes Island. On both sides of the border, there are now some twenty-two locations in new areas where Barred Owls have been sighted, from western Montana and northern Idaho to both eastern and western Washington; in addition to these movements there are two isolated records for northeastern Oregon (Taylor and Forsman 1976). In the western parts of both British Columbia and Washington these records represent an intrusion of the Barred Owl into what was formerly exclusive Spotted Owl territory, and since it seems unlikely that the eastern owl could have been there in numbers without being detected, the movement is probably as recent as the records. What happens next, when two closely related species of similar habits and requirements overlap, remains to be seen, but meanwhile the Barred Owl is abundant in woodlands from the Atlantic to the Rockies.

Once they have found a forest area or swampy woods to their liking, the Barred Owl family remains there and breeds in the same spot or even the same tree, year after year, if no woodcutter arrives. In the northern parts they seem to prefer forests of pines or hemlock, but coming south these may be mixed with hardwoods and eventually even pure stands of willow, poplar, sweet gum, and sycamore trees, or any tree which provides the large cavities Barred Owls prefer for nesting. These birds will also clean out and deepen an old hawk's nest if need be. The cavities in trees may be two feet or more in depth and usually nothing is added to the litter already on the bottom, nor do they spend much time in making an open nest more comfortable, although there are instances where a few pine needles have been added.

Barred Owls lay two or three eggs in the north, while in Florida two seems to be the standard number; incubation which takes from three to four weeks is largely a female duty although the male may at times spell his mate for brief periods and he hunts for all of her food during this time. In Florida and the Gulf states courting begins in January and by February the female will have at least one of her two eggs in the nest. In New England the nesting season begins in the middle of March and continues through April, but in both New Jersey and Iowa there are records of nesting beginning in the last week of February. While these dates are early, this owl is, in the north at least, not such an early nester as the Great Horned Owl.

Because the offspring of the Barred Owl are so few, the parents are able to give them great care and may continue feeding through the ensuing summer. After the first difficult period, if it is a nest outside on the limb of a tree, the young birds will learn to scramble about in the branches before they learn to fly, while eating is also a learned progress toward self-sufficiency, with the first food being torn into little bits and fed to them by the parents. About half of the food for this species of owl consists of mice, but it is omnivorous, plants excepted, and in addition to other mammals up to the size of weasels, it will prey on frogs, salamanders, even turtles, water snakes, and fish of various kinds. In Florida cotton and water rats, fish, crayfish and crabs are staple items in the diet. In the past Barred Owls took some poultry, but probably not as much as Great Horned Owls. They do eat other birds, including Screech and Long-eared owls; but while birds are taken in great variety they probably don't make up a considerable part of the diet unless there is no other food available, which in light of their varied tastes must rarely be the case.

The relationship of the Barred Owl to the Great Horned and Screech owls is an interesting subject on which too little has been written. Forbush notes that the Barred Owl is the most abundant large owl in New England, while the Craigheads found it rather scarce in the wood lots near Ann Arbor, Michigan (Forbush 1927) (Craighead and Craighead 1969). The reasons for scarcity in the latter place were due to the fact that these were isolated sections of wooded patches, rather than broader forests. The first township studied contained 36 square miles devoted to farms, but with a scattering of wood lots throughout. A thorough survey of this area indicated that it contained six pairs of Great Horned Owls, thirteen pairs of Screech Owls, and one pair each of Barn and Long-eared owls, but not a single pair of Barred Owls, despite the fact that they are common during winter and summer in the general area. A second plot was selected for comparison, which was one of broken hardwood stands with larger sections of woods. Here there were eight pairs of Great Horned Owls and this time three pairs of Barred Owls, but no Screech Owls.

The situation in this part of Michigan seems to be that the Great Horned Owl, which dominates the Barred Owl, does not allow the two large species to exist together when wooded patches are small, but when the habitat is more forestlike, the Barred Owl can keep out of the way in the territory of the Great Horned and still find room to raise its family. The Screech Owl gets along well in the broken farm-and-wood lot country because it can nest and roost in old apple orchards and other trees around cultivated fields which are too civilized for the Barred Owl to make its home, even though it is prone to hunt such areas. In heavily wooded areas the Barred Owl is careful to select whichever parts the Great Horned Owl wants least. If the latter has taken up the swampy area, the Barred Owls will be found on the ridges, if the countryside is divided that way. While it thus plays second fiddle to the greater and fiercer Horned Owl, the Barred Owl in turn preys upon all smaller owls, and the Screech Owl must make way for both of these big owls.

Barred Owls usually hunt at twilight, as well as during the night.

They often spend their days roosting in seclusion, but from time to time one may see them about on a cloudy day. They commonly share the same hunting area with Red-shouldered Hawks as daytime counterparts, so that between the two, rodents are given no time to rest. A quite different relationship exists between the Barred Owl and the Goshawk. When the snow is deep in the north a Goshawk will turn from easier bird prey to tackle the rival predator which equals him in power. When a Goshawk and Barred Owl match beaks and talons, victory is an uncertain thing, and oftentimes some carrion eater will have a chance to dine on the remains of both these knights.

SPOTTED OWL *(Strix occidentalis)*

Specifics: Length: 16 to 19". Wingspread: 42 to 45". Weight: 1.1
            to 1.7 lbs.
   Range: B. C. through mts. of Calif.; Rockies from Colo.
            into Mexico (see N. A. distribution map 13, p. 27).

The Spotted Owl of the West is closely related to, and in fact a
companion species with, the eastern Barred Owl, the two species occupying opposite sides of the continent. They are thus somewhat similar, but the Spotted Owl is a very shy bird by comparison and is very
seldom seen even where it is known to live. Both young and adults of
this owl are exceptionally appealing, with their dark brown eyes and
benign, rather surprised expression which makes them a favorite of
photographers. The name is a very good description of the species as
the base color is a deep brown neatly overlaid with regular white spots
on the underside; the head and hind neck also have smaller white spots,
while on the back some of these spots are ochre. The general effect is
that of a subdued tweed cloth designed to be conservative and inconspicuous. When a Spotted Owl sits close to a mottled fir trunk the bird

is scarcely visible. The head is very large with a facial disc that varies through grays and browns, depending on region, but always with darker brown concentric circles which zero in on the soft eyes. Taking the yellow out of an owl's eyes does much to also take away the fierceness of aspect. It might be mentioned here that the well-known ornithologist of New Mexico, J. Stokley Ligon (Ligon, J. S. 1961), says that the eyes are actually a very dark blue; as he has made a special study of Spotted Owls, that must be so, but the appearance is brown and there is sometimes a contrast in the shades between iris and pupil.

Like a few other owls which seldom have contact with man, this owl is quite unafraid of him and readily adapts to captivity. One ornithologist who brought a Spotted Owl home reported that it seemed to like being picked up and having its feathers affectionately stroked by him.

Until recently there were varying descriptions of the basic call of this species, but when the Spotted Owl was briefly put on the "threatened species" list of the U. S. Fish and Wildlife Service (Gould 1974) and when it was declared a "threatened species" by the state of Oregon, a number of studies and surveys were undertaken. To survey the numbers of these owls it was first necessary to record its voices on tapes, which could then be played back in the woods and the locations of answering owls noted for the survey. It turned out that Spotted Owls readily answered to their own recorded voices, but were much more difficult to call up by human imitations of their calls. Their basic call is clearly one of four hoots or syllables, given with an initial short note followed by a pause, then two more short notes followed by a longer pause, and then a final note of longer duration. This call, which takes from 2½ to 3 seconds, is transcribed as *Hoo. . .HoHoo. . . . .Hooo* (Gould 1974). There is a definite similarity to the first four notes of the closely related Barred Owl.

Sometimes the final note of the Spotted Owl's call is drawn out in a falling inflection which accents it and that version has been transcribed as *"coo---coo-coo-----coo-o-o"* (Zarn 1974a). A greater change is made when the owl skips the first note entirely, leaving a series with only three notes. The hoots which are nearest to these calls are those of the Great Horned Owl, but that call is much lower in pitch and of course has a five-note series. While both sexes of the Spotted Owl have higher pitched calls than the Horned Owl, there is a difference between the male and female when the two are calling together—the male has the lower voice.

There is something of a yelping-dog quality in even the basic call, particularly when it is heard at a distance, and a second type of call emphasizes that quality in a longer series of yelps or barks which are variable in cadence. The Spotted Owl voice one hears on the record in Peterson's "A Field Guide to Western Bird Songs" belongs to this second call. It is possible to confuse the remote yelping of a coyote with this call, but the latter is never in a series of four and coyote yelps don't remain on one pitch. One more call is notable when these owls are worried or when they warn their young; it is a brief, 1½ second whistle— whee-e-e—rising sirenlike part way through and it is more often given by the female owl.

Although the Spotted Owl is a western counterpart of the eastern Barred Owl, there is no balance between the two species in either population density or distribution. The Barred Owl is found over the eastern two thirds of the U. S. and in many places it is abundant, while the Spotted Owl has a patchy distribution at best because it is confined to specialized and often remote habitats, usually in the dense forests of mountains. During the recent survey in California which used many observers and two years of sophisticated searching only 192 pairs of these owls were located, while a similar search in Oregon resulted in the discovery of 116 pairs and 7 single owls (Forsman 1976). There are proportionately fewer records for other parts of this owl's range.

Spotted Owls are resident birds in western British Columbia, as far north as Bella Coola, with a peculiar overlap of range which may be of recent origin, where the Barred Owl intrudes along the U. S. and Canadian border as far as the coast, so that both species are found in a few areas (Taylor & Forsman 1976). In Washington State the Spotted Owl inhabits sections of heavy, old-growth (200 years or more) timber west of the crest of the Cascade Mountains. In Oregon its range in similar habitats extends somewhat east of the Cascades, to elevations of 4400 feet in Hood River County of the north to 5800 feet in Klamath County of the south (Forsman 1976). In California this owl continues down the Coast Range as far south as San Francisco Bay. In this area it occupies old groves of mature trees, usually in either Douglas fir or redwoods, where the heaviest concentrations of these owls are found in Humboldt, Siskiyou and Trinity counties. In the last named county one watershed which is 30 miles long by 6 miles wide contains sixteen pairs, which is a record for density. It is interesting that these owls are usually found quite near permanent streams or rivers, apparently because they like a cool and shaded habitat.

Along the southern coast of California there is a smaller disjunct population in the mountains from Santa Barbara County to the Laguna Mountains of San Diego County, with a few individuals sighted farther north to Monterey County. Here these owls live in dense thickets of canyon live oak, sycamore, or ponderosa pine. Yet a third isolated population in California inhabits mixed conifer groves along the western slope of the Sierra Nevada from Plumas County in the north to Kern County in the south (Gould 1974). In these mountains they are found at elevations of from 2500 to 7600 feet. In 1977 the U. S. Forest Service financed a study in the San Bernardino National Forest and graduate student James C. Cook turned up 26 pairs of Spotted Owls in that mountain range.

In Colorado the Spotted Owl is found in the foothill area east of the Front Range and in all of the mountains of the central and southern part of the state (Zarn 1974a). In New Mexico it is also recorded in all of the higher mountains from Taos and the Sangre de Cristo, Jemez, Mogollon, Black, and San Mateo ranges to the Guadalupe Mountains which extend into west Texas (Ligon, J. S. 1961). In this region it inhabits the densest fir and spruce forests, often where there are steep canyons and cliffs with caves or crevices for nesting. Here it nests at elevations from 6500 to 9000 feet, remaining at whatever elevation and location it calls home for both summer and winter. As elsewhere, this owl wanders little. There are regular records from southern Utah and the wooded portions of northern and eastern Arizona where the Spotted Owl is uncommon in mountainous stands of Douglas fir or yellow pine. In the Santa Rita and Catalina mountains of south-central Arizona these owls inhabit pine-oak woodland as well as higher forests (Marshall 1957). There are isolated sightings in Glacier National Park, Montana, but these are questioned as possibly due to confusion with the Barred Owl. South of the border it extends to central Mexico.

The studies made in Arizona indicate that Spotted Owls hunt over territories of about one square mile and that they only live in areas free of the Great Horned Owl. In California it has been determined that they need from 300 to 600 acres of suitable, untouched habitat—the latter figure being just under a square mile. Where these owls are relatively numerous the pairs will be spread out at 1½ to 2 mile intervals (Gould 1974). Since there were only 192 pairs located in California, it is evident that these are widely scattered throughout the state. However, since replacement individuals are needed for pair formation, these owls are never found in isolated pairs and are rarely more than 5 or 6 miles apart. As a result, pairs tend to be close together with individual concentrations of pairs widely separated. In part this is because most suitable habitat has been cut by loggers, but if these owls can live only where there are no Great Horned Owls nearby, that too may be a limiting factor, and Great Horned Owls invade newly logged areas. However, I know of an instance in California where from a single listening post a Spotted Owl, several Screech Owls, and more than one Great Horned Owl could be heard calling from various distances on the same night, indicating there is more to be learned about inter-owl tolerance.

Spotted Owls have a powerful flight and a neck long enough to let them observe the ground beneath and behind during the course of a hunting flight, allowing them to locate wood rats, deer mice, squirrels and the like. Insects also have a place in the diet of this species, as one owl collected by a scientist had nothing but noctuid moths (also called owlet moths) in its stomach, while in Oregon it is reported that a nocturnal cricket, which filled the night with its sounds, also filled the stomach of one of these strictly nocturnal owls. A detailed study in Oregon indicates that mammals make up 90%, by weight, of the diet, with flying squirrels and wood rats—which can be snatched from tree trunks and limbs at night—providing the largest part. Birds, especially Steller's Jays and small owls, contributed just over 4% of the total food weight (Forsman 1976). Bats have appeared in the stomachs of some specimens taken for museums and Joe T. Marshall, Jr. assumes that this owl can take some of them on the wing. In the same specimens and in nearby pellets belonging to this species, flying squirrels were important and at least two songbirds, an Evening Grosbeak and a Red-breasted Nuthatch were found.

In California the records for Spotted Owl nests with eggs in them run from March 1 to the 10th of May, with the slightly off-white eggs laid mainly in the last week of March. New Mexico records, at 7000 feet, are not much later than that since most of them are around April 4 (Ligon, J. S. 1926). In Oregon these nests are from 65 to 151 feet high in hollows of top-blasted conifers, which are usually trees some 200 to 380 years old. As the top breaks are jagged, there are often projections above the nest, or new growth. Therefore, sometimes the hollow is entered through a hole in the trunk (Forsman 1976). Similar sites are used in New Mexico, but in that state crevices and caves in cliffs are also utilized, and one such cavern nest was improved with dry sticks and twigs and lined with bark, twigs and feathers, which is more home improvement than most owls are prone to use. Many accounts of this owl's nest in southern California also refer to cliff cavity nesting, but the stump ends of old oak and sycamore are also used and as everywhere in its range the Spotted Owl lays two, or occasionally three, eggs.

Only the female Spotted Owl engages in the incubation while the male feeds her regularly and both parents care for the two chicks which are blind for the first five to nine days. At about the age of thirty-five days the owlets leave their nest in a most percipitous manner—quite literally by falling. Since they are not really able to fly at this stage the downward descent is a fluttering drop with frantic grasps toward limbs or twigs that may arrest, for the moment at least, the downward plunge. The owlets are not injured by the drop and soon climb up the undergrowth to a perch a few feet above the forest floor where the parents continue to feed and care for them. Perhaps they are easier to feed down near the source of food supply, which consists of small mammals, insects and medium-sized birds, and there they remain until ready to fly at the age of six weeks. Whatever the reason, this method gives the owlet special care on a one to one basis, which may be necessary for the continuance of this species of owl which has such a slight hold on its place in the natural world.*

*For more on the Spotted Owl as a "unique" or "threatened" species see "Afterword," pp. 184 - 188.

GREAT GRAY OWL *(Strix nebulosa)*

Specifics: Length: 24 to 33". Wingspread: 48 to 60". Weight: 1.7 to
3.3 lbs.

Range: Alaska, Canada, Mont., Wyo., Idaho, Calif. Mts. (see
N. A. distribution map 14, p. 27). Boreal N. of
Europe and Asia.

One of the older names for this bird was "spectral owl," and
its present scientific name also carries the implication of something
dark, misty and perhaps not quite defined. These implications apply
not to the physical bird, despite the nondescript dusky-gray plumage
marked with darker stripes, nor to its size because it is the largest of all
our owls and has as much as a five-foot wingspread, but they apply rather to its presence. It is very rarely seen in the United States, even in
those parts of the Sierra Nevada of California where it is known to be
resident. Therefore, the bird watcher seldom hunts for this owl, but
waits for the owl to find him. A probably typical encounter of this
nature was described from the eastern side of the Sierras, where the
Great Gray Owl had never before been reported (Billeb 1962). A group

of young men had camped for two weeks in August at the 8700 foot level, among lodgepole pine, red fir and mountain hemlock, where the first indication of the owl was an unfamiliar *hoo*-ing in predawn darkness. A few days later a huge owl was seen flying along the same ridge, but the bird was extremely cautious and made no sound. Again, the men were awakened at 5:00 a.m. by two owls calling to one another —apparently opposite sexes, since the pitch of each call was different. A few minutes passed, and one of these birds flew overhead—perching in a pine some thirty yards distant where its imposing figure could be picked up in a lantern beam and positively identified as a Great Gray Owl.

Another observer, this time in Yosemite National Park—where for a number of years, the Great Gray Owl has been regularly, if uncommonly seen—had more luck. He was simply driving along a road in the park during daylight when he spotted one of these owls perched atop a small fir tree in the center of a wet meadow. Since the bird was some sixty yards away it could be observed through binoculars. Notably, in flight its long curving tail distinguished it, even at a distance, from the Great Horned Owl. At that range the lack of ear tufts on the Great Gray was not noticeable. The only other observation made was that the owl was soon mobbed by a group of chickadees, warblers and kinglets (Dixon 1944). In Yosemite National Park Great Grays nest and are regularly seen at two points: around the meadow at Bridalveil Campground at 7000 feet, and near the meadow at Crane Flat at 6200 feet, both sites being in the Canadian zone. Nesting is later here than in Canada or Wyoming, with eggs apparently laid in May and young fledged in July. Individuals of the species have been observed in the Yosemite area as low as 4000 feet, especially in fall and winter. Elsewhere in California mountains these owls are extremely rare with only two records from farther north in the period 1954 through 1977.

A Great Gray Owl looks something like the Barred Owl, which is a close relative belonging to the same genus, but it is a far larger bird with an overall length of two and a half feet or more, including a splendid broad tail a foot long. The eyes of the Great Gray are a bright yellow, as opposed to the dark of the Barred Owl, and the head is the largest of any owl and shows striking concentric rings in the facial discs. This bird is dusky-gray, as the name implies, mottled with an equally dusky black and grayish-white on its uppersides. The darker streaks on its underparts are notably vertical in arrangement. Whereas the Great Gray Owl seems large and heavy enough to take game the size of a hare or a grouse, one of the ghostly things about the bird is that it is not nearly as heavy-bodied as it seems. Much of the bulk is actually made up of several inches of long, lax feathers, under which is a trim body of considerably less weight than that of either the Great Horned or the Snowy Owl.

Its voice fits the great size of the bird, being a deep, booming *who-hooo-hooo*, which differs from the Great Horned Owl's call by its lack of regularity. Sometimes it will have only one note, or there will be four notes; again the bird may call softly in a firm sigh with an *oooh* rather than a hoot. These calls and the great owls which utter them belong to the boreal northland, within all the tree limits of Alaska, then eastward across wooded Canada to Quebec, but the distribution is heavily weighted westward and the breeding range does not extend that far east. Curiously enough it is, as we have noted, a breeding resident of the mountain forests of central California, as well as the northern Rockies. In winter it also strays south from Canada. The Great Gray Owl has been seen regularly in the Adirondack Park area of New York, and more rarely in New Jersey and Pennsylvania. There are also records from Michigan and Wisconsin, while in some winters the Great Gray Owl is fairly common in central Minnesota. In the winter of 1976-77 Great Gray Owls were sighted at Ashland and Orono, Maine, and in the West at Kalispell, Montana, as well as their normal haunts in the mountains of California. Sightings in Montana are occasional and in winter, but the Craigheads have studied a breeding pair in Wyoming (Craighead & Craighead 1969), so there may be other pairs hidden away in the Canadian zones of Idaho or elsewhere. In Washington and Oregon it is again present as a winter migrant.

It was calculated that the pair observed by the Craigheads in Wyoming would have started to lay about the first of April, with incubation completed by the end of that month and the resulting brood of fledglings ready to depart their nest—which was one borrowed from a hawk—around June 8th. In Alaska the egg dates are through May, June, and even July. There are usually three eggs to a clutch and these eggs are quite small considering the size of the adult bird. In Wyoming it was possible to calculate the size of territory covered by a pair of Great Gray Owls in the course of their hunting. This proved to be an irregular area enclosing about a square mile, within which was everything they needed. Other raptors had territories which adjoined that of the owls, but these did not overlap significantly, indicating that diurnal hawks were not welcome in the same space.

For the Great Gray Owl, hunting is by preference crepuscular (during twilight), though of course in the far northern summer hunting has to be done by daylight. Pellets from the Wyoming pair yielded the following dietary statistics: meadow mice 66.3%; pocket gophers 27.7%; and red squirrels 3.6%. There were also the remains of weasels, and shrews, with 1.0% being small birds. Like their close relative the Spotted Owl, the Great Grays improve their nests by lining them with small sticks, mosses and feathers, and there is some, perhaps dubious, evidence that they make their own at times, though most are based on old hawk nests. The young birds are said, by the few lucky enough to have seen them, to be most friendly toward man, which follows the pattern set by Barred Owls of the same genus.

From the small number of records of sightings of these owls, as compared to the Snowy Owl for example, it can be seen that the Great Gray is an aloof as well as scarce owl. The owl figured on Color Plate XII was found by a combination of searching and luck when, toward the end of one October, Don Phillips set off in company with a moose-hunting friend to explore the wildlife of Quebec in that season.

At Senneterre they picked up an Indian guide and canoed north-ward along the lake to the point at which the Bell River begins to send its waters toward James Bay. Where the river flows out of the lake, there is a cabin for the use of anyone who reaches that isolated point, so the travelers made this their central camp. Growth in the area con-sists of tight groves of spruce which are interwoven with ambling moose trails that serve for men as well as for their game. After following one of these paths wherever it led, in a company of Gray Jays, grouse, juncos, and Boreal Chickadees, the woods suddenly opened out into a grassy patch. In the center of this stood a pine and there in the midday sun, perched, unperturbed and motionless, was a Great Gray Owl. It had not been expected at that point in that season, but then the owl hadn't ex-pected the observer either. Phillips had brought no sketch pad that day, so he simply sat down and mentally took in all of the aspects of this owl which an artist would need for painting a likeness. For two hours he watched and as this particular owl had lived far from the world of men, possibly never having seen a human before, it took no notice and dozed away on its perch. When the afternoon became full, Phillips carefully backed away from the clearing and that evening translated his observations into sketches and notes. The most notable thing about this owl was the seeming excess of feathers around the body, with layer on layer of plumes overlapping. In October this insulation was not needed, but a month or two later in the same area or northwestward, such insulation would allow the owl to hunt in comfort through the blasts of midwinter.

Since the Great Gray is nowhere common and in many parts of its range the rarest of owls, the only method for learning its ways is to locate an area where it appears with regularity. One such region is in southeastern Manitoba, from Lac du Bonnet down to northern Minnesota, where its preferred habitat of black spruce and tamarack bogs is nearly continuous. There, studies were begun in 1968 by Robert W. Nero, of the Wildlife Programs of the Manitoba Dept. of Renewable Resources and Transportation Services, and other interested observers who worked mostly on their own time and at temperatures to thirty below zero. Work came first because Great Grays use old hawk or crow nests which are often so dilapidated that they collapse, spilling eggs or chicks onto the snow. Also, there are areas of good habitat which simply have no old nests available. Mr. Nero thought of building secure platforms based on wire mesh with bowls of cedar boughs and tamarack twigs. Presently there are sixty of these foundations and three of the five built last winter were successfully used by the owls for nesting (Nero, *in litt.*).

Because the Great Gray is the most elusive of large owls, unless driven into the settled areas by food shortages, the man-made nests were not only useful to the birds, but they also made observations possible throughout the nesting season. A "wanted" poster picturing the huge owl was circulated, with a text seeking information on the owl. This effort, which had the support of the Manitoba government, asked anyone who spotted a Great Gray Owl in any season to report his sighting to the nearest Conservation Officer or to one of the four interested owlsmen listed at the bottom of the poster. Among the latter was Michael Collins, a graduate student in zoology at the University of Manitoba who was making a detailed study for his thesis. The bog in which Collins patiently watched a nesting pair of owls, sometimes around the clock, through the fledgling stage of the young, was much like the one where Phillips observed the bird in eastern Canada.

In this studied region in southeastern Manitoba, a mated pair of Great Grays normally takes over an old nest, as early as mid-February, 15 to 35 feet high in a deciduous tamarack tree. By the end of March or early April the female lays from two to five eggs which require thirty days for incubation. The nesting season thus extends from a possibly sub-zero wintry beginning, to the hot, humid days of June when the young are still being fed. The male bird is exclusively a hunter, and he brings home a variety of mice, including the red-backed voles which are staples of the family diet. Only if mice become scarce in the bogs do these owls venture out into the open, where, having no fear of man, they may perch even near settlements in the northland. Normally they remain in remote sections and return to the same nest year after year.

Mr. Nero and his colleagues have banded both young and older owls to determine age at first breeding and the sporadic movements of Great Grays. These welcomed studies will increase our future knowledge of the biology of this great owl. Nothing, however, will diminish the awesome presence of this aloof hunter with a five-foot wingspread, dusky plumage, slow-deliberate flight, and a desire for privacy which is so adamant that one will most often know of the owl's presence only from a *whoop* or a *who-oops*, called out from forest depths.

GREAT GRAY IN FLIGHT, BACKDROP OF SNOW   *(Photo courtesy of Robert R. Taylor)*

LONG-EARED OWL *(Asio otus)*

Specifics: Length: 13 to 16". Wingspread: 36 to 43". Weight: 6.5 to 12 ozs.

Range: U. S. except Alaska; S. Canada; Europe through central Asia (see N. A. distribution map 15, p. 28).

Across America there are two woodland owls of considerable size which have prominent "horns." It is inevitable that the Long-eared and Great Horned Owl stand together for some initial comparisons because their feather tufts, whether we call these "ears" or "horns," amount to the same headdress. The Screech Owl of the same habitat also has these tufts, but it is recognizably very much smaller than the two large owls. Of the major pair, the Horned is considerably larger, although in some lights that might not be immediately apparent, and it presents a bulky, broad-shouldered appearance. The Long-eared Owl is slimmer as well as lighter, with narrow wings, and it can in no way project the bearing of massive power that the Horned Owl radiates. The Long-eared Owl is not only slim to begin with, but it also has a further capacity of elongating its body and tightening up the middle until it presents to the world a compressed cylinder of as little as two and a half inches in diameter. The point of this odd posture is to look as much as possible like some dead stub of a tree limb, and it succeeds very well in the act since its overall markings are a nondescript olive-brown in the East, or a mottled white and dusky in the West, a grayish effect that matches tree bark very well.

As for these feather tufts, those on the Long-eared Owl are slim, an inch long rather than the two inches of the larger owl; they are set closer together on the head, and held straight up or slightly curved when perched—the Horned Owl often cocks his to the sides. Both owls tend to flatten these tufts when in flight.

A Long-eared Owl has white eyebrows under these tufts and a white moustache around its beak, but lacks the distinctive white ruff around the throat and upper breast of the Horned Owl. Perhaps the readiest distinction between the two birds is that the underparts of the Long-eared Owl are mottled and streaked, while on the larger owl they are rather finely cross-barred. The flight of the Long-eared Owl is very buoyant, due largely to the ratio of wing area to its light body weight. When seen as a shadow against a moonlit night sky, this owl glides and circles, or hovers if something living is spotted below. When perched, its folded wings are longer than the tail.

The Long-eared is a strictly nocturnal owl and like the Horned Owl a resident of forests and wood-

LONG-EARED IN CYLINDRICAL POSE

lands, but although the two owls often occupy the same general area the greater owl completely dominates and will make a meal of the Long-eared Owl if the opportunity arises. This encourages the lesser predator to hunt in separate places, such as clearings outside the forest itself. In many areas this is a very common owl, but it is so secretive that few people see one of the birds unless it is struck by an auto, which is probably the greatest hazard for all owls these days. Most Long-eared Owls are resident where found, but in winter some will make a southward shift and those that do so gather in flocks of ten or twenty owls for their journey. It is in this season that they are found in the Gulf states. In the West there seems to be no real migration, with perhaps only some shifting to better areas and lower levels in winter.

Elevation may be a significant factor locally in the distribution of this species, but over larger areas it is not. For example, in California west of the Sierra Nevadas the Long-eared Owl is a bird of the Upper Sonoran zone and not found above 2000 feet, while in the Rockies it breeds much higher; there are records there for 7500, and even 10,000 feet in New Mexico. These records are what one would expect for a bird that breeds in the northern U. S. and southern Canada, but it is obviously a flexible bird in habitat as it has also been found nesting in the Organ-Pipe Cactus National Monument in Arizona and has become an abundant nester in the foothills around Tombstone (Phillips et. al. 1964). So it is only in the North that it is an owl of dense conifer forests, or in the Southeast in pine woods. In Nevada it is a bird of the pinyon-juniper scrubland, while in California it selects the riparian woodland of willows and cottonwoods, where these still exist, or the oak and grassland savannahs that occupy so much of the hilly parts of the state.

One reason for these diverse habitats is this owl's appetite for rats and mice which in the West and Southwest occupy different environments. From moist meadows these owls can get meadow mice (*Microtus*), harvest mice (*Reithrodontomys*), and pocket gophers (*Thomomys*), while from drier habitats there are the kangaroo rats (*Dipodomys*), deer mice (*Peromyscus*) and pack rats (*Neotoma*), or other nocturnal rodents (Johnson 1954). Cottontail rabbits have some importance in the diet, but not nearly so much so as with the Horned Owl; beetles, their grubs and other insect food, as well as frogs, are taken in certain places, not in others. A recent survey of world-wide information on

Long-eared Owl prey indicated that in North America two genera of mice, *Microtus* (meadow) and *Peromyscus* (white-footed) made up 82% of the food taken, with birds only 1.7% (Marti 1976). This specialized feeding is at the opposite pole from the diet of the Screech Owl.

Secretiveness is the Long-eared Owl's best protection from man, but when found they are not always alarmed by man's presence and a female may sit tight on the nest until approached within a few feet. If surprised on the nest or while taking small game, they have a fierce looking defensive reaction of spreading their wings and distending each feather to form great arches over their hissing heads. When nesting among cottonwoods in California the Long-eared Owl will select an old crow or magpie nest which they then use as a platform, adding some small twigs, leaves, and down-feathers plucked from the female's belly. If no such platform is at hand, they will pile the sticks in the crotch of a tree. Also, I recall one nest that was "built" in a pothole of a dry wash's bank, since trees were practically nil in that locale, and crows, which will break up the household of these owls, had appropriated all arboreal spots. Eggs are laid as early as March 13 in central California, with April the prime month for laying the four or five eggs. There are similar records across the country, with later May and June dates for higher elevations in New Mexico.

Except during nesting season these are owls on the quiet side and one is more likely to spot them flying past as shadows on a moonlit night than to hear their hoot, which is softer than the Horned Owl and without cadence. Sometimes they moan a little, or when disturbed they will utter a three-syllable *wuk-wuk-wuk*! In some places this species is called the "cat owl" because it does make sounds like the nocturnal threats of a domestic cat which is deciding whether to fight or not. Like a number of other owls, hissing and beak-snapping are common responses if one is near and sometimes, it is said, they will give out with a series of shrieks, but that is certainly not common in the West. Despite all of these possibilities in the way of multiple voices, one can live in close harmony with these mousers and never hear a thing from them.

SHORT-EARED OWL *(Asio flammeus)*

Specifics: Length: 13 to 17". Wingspread: 38 to 44". Weight: 7 to 17 ozs.

Range: U. S. & Canada; to cent. Mex. in winter; much of S. America; Europe and northern Asia (see N. A. distribution map 16, p. 28).

The Short-eared Owl is a close relative of the previous species, but differs from it by a distinct choice of habitat and by habits which suit it to that choice. Where the Long-eared Owl is a forest bird in most places, this species shuns dense woods or any woods at all, and has moved into open marshes and prairie grasslands. Short-eared Owls like saltwater marshes just as much as those which are fresh and they will inhabit coastal dunes just as readily as open grasslands. Since there are few or no trees in these habitats, their favored perching places are where the grasses form high clumps or among the tules on wetlands. While these owls are the same mousers as their relatives, they have diverged from the strictly nocturnal habits of the Long-eared Owl and hunt for meadow mice in late afternoons, or all day if the weather is cloudy. [For a complete study see: (Clark 1975).]

The odds against this most useful owl have been stacked in recent years, as they have no defense against the kind of attack man has subjected them to. Long-eared Owls have been bothered very little by man since they are so secretive and nocturnal. Not so the Short-eared Owl, which inhabits the same marshes duck hunters frequent and at least until recently duck hunters almost invariably shot the owls on sight—just because they present a moving target; certainly there is no sport in hitting a slow-flying owl which presents no danger to waterfowl, even though in nesting season it may bother the nestlings of Black-necked Stilts or an occasional Common Snipe. An even more devastating attack came with the draining and cultivation of so much of the wetlands in the Midwest and Far West. When these open fields were planted to alfalfa or grain, the owls could still use them to some extent, but other crops or grains, like corn, made them unsuitable and in the Southwest, with the depletion of grassland by grazing, these owls have taken to hunting under thickets of chaparral growing on foothills or in canyons, which is a quite different habitat from former rank grasslands.

The Short-eared Owl often shares its chosen habitat with a pair of Marsh Hawks, which it resembles in tawny color but differs from in having a short tail and no white rump patch. Both birds spend much of their time flying close to the ground in search of prey. The flight of the Marsh Hawk, unlike the owl's, is an even glide over the hunting ground, while the owl flaps its wings and, when a meal is spotted below, either hovers in the air or dips down and picks up its prey without arresting its flight. The best distinction between these two birds is that the owl has buffy patches on the underwings and an oblong black patch at the carpal or wrist joint of the wings—these markings stand out even at a considerable distance.

Short-eared Owls are not as streamlined as their close relatives the Long-eared Owls and they lack the heavy dark markings of the latter, while the ear-tufts are rudimentary and seldom raised, so one is not likely to notice them. The color of individual owls varies, but if one thinks in terms like buffy, tawny, and tan, that is the color range. Less often there will be a grayish tone. Whatever the ground color, the shaft of most feathers has a darker, often rusty-brown stripe. The facial discs of these owls vary from dusky to dark brown, with the black rims around the bird's bright lemon-yellow eyes presenting a striking contrast.

The Short-eared Owl's nesting site is quite a departure from most other owls in that it is neither in a tree or a cavity, but on the surface of the ground where it is concealed only by a little grass or, in some cases, rushes. Usually the spot is well hidden from a casual observer. The birds pluck a few feathers of the downy sort from themselves to line the open nest. The courtship is quite extraordinary, being more like that of a lark than an owl (Dubois 1924). The male courts his mate by pursuing her while voicing a series of melodious toots—not worthy of a lark to be sure, but the best an owl can do. Then, which is even more like a lark, the male will rise to great heights of two or three hundred feet before plunging into a steep dive. At intervals as he plunges the male will bring his wings together beneath him, clapping them to make a sound which can be heard from the ground. When this courtship is successful, as it is likely to be since these owls are thought to mate for life, the female will lay from four to nine eggs in a nest which may be anywhere from the tundra on the Arctic slope of Alaska to southern California west of the deserts. In the East it breeds as far south as New Jersey, northern Ohio and Indiana, and locally in Kansas.

The grassy hollow in which the young are hatched is soon trampled flat, leaving a huddle of young owls on the ground. Since incubation begins after the second egg is laid, the owlets will vary in age. The youngest will still be downy when the eldest displays his first contour feathers. During this period the male will find some nearby perch from which he may act as a guardian for his mate and their young, and he has his means of defense well thought out in advance. Should a skunk or a coyote pass nearby, he goes into the injured wing act, dropping into the grass near the intruder and fluttering about, pretending to be an easy victim. At other times the trick will be to fly to the ground at a good distance and utter a cry like a captured mouse, which is sure to bring the interloper over to steal the prey. Even the nestlings of this owl have tricks to play. When one is caught out in the open, it will roll over and play dead so effectively that it will appear so even if picked up. How much good that might do against a coyote is doubtful, but if the whole group perform the same act it could save most of them.

Eight or nine owlets in a huddle on the ground are too many for safety, so the process is for the oldest nestling to wander a few feet away from the nest, while still being fed by the parents. As time passes the distance becomes greater and greater until some of them will be as much as a hundred yards away, with all of the siblings scattered in different directions and distances, even before they are able to fly. All of this time the parents know the exact whereabouts of each one and they continue to feed them at the rate of one mouse per owlet per meal. Always they are ready to swing down with the broken-wing act or some other trick if a threat appears. As the young grow larger, hunting continues in something of a family group which may hold more or less together through the first winter. Even before nesting season a male and female may hunt together, although not as a team.

Sometimes when food is extremely abundant a large gathering of Short-eared Owls will come to the same spot for a communal hunt. One of the biggest of these concourses was described by my father, John G. Tyler, from the turn of the century, at a time when wildlife was still abundant, even where men had moved in (Tyler 1913). The place in central California was the stubblefield left after a wheat harvest, where mice had congregated in fearful numbers. He wrote, "I was astonished at the great number of Short-eared Owls, Barn Owls, and Marsh Hawks that appeared just before sundown and began hunting over the fields. The number of doves that were disturbed by these raptors was almost beyond belief, and the noise made by their wings as they flew away was almost deafening. When I resumed my walk toward camp it seemed a really perilous journey, and there was grave danger of being struck by one of the rapidly flying doves that wheeled and turned, alighted and took wing again in a veritable maze. I estimated that there were at least two hundred Short-eared Owls in sight. They could easily be distinguished from the Barn Owls by the marked resemblance of their flight to that of the Texas Nighthawk."

A generation later we never found this owl in any numbers even in the same area. Wheat fields had given way to orchards and vineyards and the Short-eared Owl nests were hard to find in April in the marshy ground where the San Joaquin River overflowed in the spring runoff.

In California, as in many other places there are two populations of these owls, one of residents which spend their entire life within the same county, and a second much larger population made up of winter migrants. While these owls can hunt over the snow farther north, many of them migrate southward to escape harsh weather and in winter these migrants travel as far as central Mexico, Baja California and the islands off the Mexican coast. Apparently the Short-eared Owls of the eastern U. S. are somewhat less migratory in habits. In what has been said so far about this owl the only mention of its voice was the soft nuptial tooting song and its imitation of a mouse's squeak. That is because, for most of the year at least, it is a quiet bird. It does have a clucking note for its young and its major call is a barking note—a *wow* repeated perhaps eight times, then a pause before continuing. There are also some growls and whines, but not in a class with the cat noises of its relative the Long-eared Owl. Its hearing, however, is equal to that species, the ear having an opening two inches long which occupies all of the available space. With these it can hear a distant mouse shaking a blade of grass, or the footfalls of a beetle lumbering along invisibly.

SHORT-EARED OWLS FAVOR PERCHING PLACES WHERE GRASSES FORM HIGH CLUMPS. *(Photo by Anne Kutz)*

BOREAL OWL *(Aegolius funereus)*

Specifics: Length: 8 to 12". Wingspread: 19 to 25". Weight: 3 to 6 ozs.

Range: wooded Alaska & Canada; N. & cent. Europe; N. & cent. Asia (see N. A. distribution map 17, p. 29).

The Boreal Owl is about the same size as the common Screech Owl, but it lacks ear tufts. Its attire is a rich chocolate brown, sometimes showing tawny, which is spotted all over in white, with the spots small and dense on the crown and largest along the scapulars (shoulders). Its facial discs are light, usually washed with brown and surrounded by a darker brown border. Since the head, eyes, and yellow beak are all large, its aspect is the solemn essence of owlness. The voice, on the other hand, is most unowllike with never a trace of a hoot. From its deep forest haunts the Boreal Owl gives out a liquid sound which suggests dripping water, or some have registered the notes as a bell-like *ting, ting, ting*.

For those U. S. bird watchers who wish to see this tamest of owls, a trip to the wooded sections of Canada is almost a necessity. These birds wander into the northern portions of the U. S. only in small numbers in winter, with some exceptions which will be noted later. Don Phillips, who likes his nature whole, made a trip to the Gaspé Peninsula of Quebec, to collect butterflies, photograph the nests of Blackburnian and other warblers, to check out the Labrador subspecies of the Horned Owl, and hopefully to see the less common Boreal Owl. He and his wife had begun the climb to the top of Mont Albert in Gaspensian Provincial Park toward the tableland at the top. The trail led up through lichen-covered trees along the Sainte-Anne River. While walking in the wake of a Spruce Grouse, they came to a ravine where water cascaded over some mossy rocks that invited a side excursion along the stream. There, after a few steps, they came face to face with two golden eyes staring at them from a dusky feathered, perfectly round face. As expected, this Boreal Owl showed no fear of the humans intruding into his private forest. He cocked his head from side to side until satisfied with his own observations, then silently glided downward without a quiver of his wings, then upwards—and out of sight into the treetops.

The same observers first found the young of this owl while looking for sapsucker nests in the forested parts of New Brunswick. After stopping for the evening camp, Phillips made a broad circuit, pounding on all trees that contained holes and after tapping on a number of them with a stick, one likely looking sapsucker hole produced not that bird, but a wide-eyed Boreal Owl which sat patiently for a sketch. After this parent had left, Phillips put his hand down the hole, which was seven feet above the ground, and took out the three chicks—but only after he had returned to the car for gloves. These three owlets were a dark chocolate color, indicating that they were at least two to three weeks old since they have white down until that time. There were a few white spots on the forehead, the facial discs, and on the center of the breast. After sketching the chicks to compare them with the juvenal plumage of the Saw-whet Owlets, they were returned to the nest (see illustration on next page).

For those who can't make the trip to Canada, the best place to look for Boreal Owls in the East is in the northeastern counties of Maine and in northern Vermont where these owls seem to be resident. For western birders, central Alberta is the most certain breeding area where these owls can be seen, but there is also some evidence of a relict breeding population in the spruce-fir-lodgepole pine forest of Larimer County, in north-central Colorado (Baldwin & Koplin 1966). That area is entirely separated from the northern breeding regions, but as there is a similarly isolated refuge in the Old World, far south of the normal range of this circumpolar bird, the possibility is plausible enough, and in any case the Boreal Owl is in Colorado over a long season. In wintertime this owl moves southward in numbers, as in the 1968-69 invasion of southern Ontario. It strays south of the Canadian border from Idaho, Montana, South Dakota, northeastern Wisconsin, northern Ohio, to New England, from where it is sometimes a straggler as far south as Connecticut and Pennsylvania.

Because the Boreal Owl is so tame that it can sometimes be picked up without protest, the story has circulated that by day it is blind or at least has very poor eyesight. While this owl seems to avoid bright sunlight and stays in dense timber, and may readily be blinded by bright light from a flashlight, the story can't be true since in the Alaskan taiga this owl perforce hunts by day during the Arctic summer when the sun never sets. Elsewhere it is strictly a nocturnal hunter and for night hunt-

---

YOUNG OWLS HAVE DIFFERENT PLUMAGE FROM THEIR PARENTS
Left Boreal; **Right** Saw-whet

Don
Phillips

ing both the Boreal and Saw-whet owls have completely modified hearing adaptations. Their skulls are so specialized to allow for the asymmetry of the inner ear, that if seen without the covering feathers they seem misshapen, as indeed they are if symmetry is taken as norm, but for the purposes of exactly locating its prey by means of sound, this irregular shape has the advantages described earlier in Part 1 of this book.

Boreal Owls do not try for an early start on their breeding season as do the Great Horned Owls, whose young are large and slow maturing. Boreals begin their egg laying in mid-April and continue through May. From three to seven eggs, with four being the usual number, are laid in an old woodpecker or sapsucker cavity or, once in a while, outside in an abandoned nest—not of crow- or hawk-size. Strewn about the cavity nest found by Phillips in June were the remains of meadow mice (*Microtus*) and several small perching birds. Since this owl is a night hunter, these birds are probably located by the noises they make near the owl's roosting place. The number of actual songbirds taken is thought to be minimal (Bent 1961, p. 223), and to correspond to the Boreal Owl's nesting season. Mice (further north, lemmings) and insects are their staple food items. The few studies of available pellets indicate the Arctic white-footed mouse (*Peromyscus*), meadow mice, and redback voles (*Clethrionomys*) are also common food items. In confirmation of this diet, experiments have demonstrated that adult Boreal Owls would leave sparrows alone when they were put in with the caged owl, if mice were presented to them at the same time.

When it comes to winter feeding on top of snow-covered ground, the Boreal Owl is at a disadvantage compared to a large owl like the Snowy. The bigger owl can take animals as large as the Arctic hare, which is exposed as are ptarmigan and other grouse, or it can feed on water birds. For the small Boreal Owl there are no insects in winter and it lacks the power to take the larger animals and birds, so when the crust of the snow is frozen over, protecting the mice in their homes, food may become scarce and at such times a few strays have wandered as far south as Oregon or Pennsylvania. One might expect these southward movements more often, and with more of these owls, but the fact is that as a rule mice don't like being locked in under the snow for long. After they have been confined for a few days they are prone to nibble through the surface ice and come out on top. There, they are perfect targets for Boreal Owls which can hear their tiny feet running along an icy crust.

SAW-WHET OWL *(Aegolius acadicus)*

Specifics: Length: 7 to 8.5". Wingspread: 17 to 21". Weight: 2 to 4 ozs.

Range: S. Canada, U. S., except South; to southern Mexico (see N. A. distribution map 18, p. 29).

While the Boreal Owl is found all around the world in northern latitudes, its close relative, the Saw-whet Owl, is restricted to North America. It ranges mostly south of the previous owl's homeland, overlapping into southern Canada and along our northern border. Within the United States it is absent from the southern states, except on rare occasions. In the East this is the smallest species of owl, easily distinguished from the Screech Owl by the lack of ear tufts. In the West, where there are several small species, the Pygmy Owl, whose range and habitat overlap with it in a number of places, is the most likely bird to be confused with the Saw-whet Owl. Where the Pygmy has the black, false-eye marks on the back of its neck, the Saw-whet has only white spots, and while the head of the Pygmy Owl is small, the Saw-whet has a very large round head for the size of its body. It is also strictly nocturnal, while

(Saw-whet Owl continued on page 177)

Don Phillips
Sept. 1975

Don Phillips
SEPT. 1975

the Pygmy Owl hunts by day.

In the northern part of its range the Saw-whet Owl is distinguished from the Boreal Owl by its smaller size, by having a black beak (Boreal has yellow), and by the less broad and less distinct black margin around the facial discs. The uppersides of the Saw-whet Owl are a rich, reddish-brown with some white spotting on the wings, while the underside is white with blotchy streaks of red-brown. The facial discs are a dusky white, and the short tail is a dark gray-brown with narrow white bars and a white margin at the tip. The expression of this little owl is fixed by the white patch between—and v-ing up over—the eyes, which gives it a look of wide-eyed bemusement at all times.

Capt. Bendire (Bendire 1892) called the Saw-whet Owl "stupid," since it would let his men pick up one of the birds by hand and bring it into camp. It has surprisingly little fear of men and will gladly accept nesting boxes if these are placed in trees which have a good mouse run close by, even if they are near human habitation. Despite being tolerant of men, the Saw-whet is a very shy bird for the most part and one that likes to keep to itself in a dense thicket or in heavy coniferous forests. But it shows some curiosity about intruding campers and may even come up to a night campfire to see what is happening in *its* private forest. In California it was assumed for a long time that the Saw-whet, as in the East, was limited to the heavy coniferous growth which is concentrated in the Sierra Nevada Mountains or in the San Bernardino Mountains to the south, where there were a number of records for this owl. These areas were in the Transition and even Canadian life zones, so when a few sightings near sea level in the San Francisco Bay Area were recorded, these were assumed to be the result of migrations of Saw-whets from the mountains toward the areas of a milder winter climate. However, it was soon proved that these lowland Saw-whet Owls actually occupied oak savannahs quite unlike the mountain forests, and did live there the year-round and that they bred in suitable woodpecker holes of the Coast Range slopes and valleys (Santee and Granfield 1939).

Some years back I became very good friends with a pair of these owls which were living on a large coastal dairy where the pastures were in the lowlands along a creek, the barns being situated on a knoll. The cattle were driven up through pastures and lanes, the hundred-odd head thoroughly stirring up the mouse and other rodent populations as they advanced to a large holding corral outside the milking barn. Early one morning in the artificially lighted darkness, I was attracted by an unusual sound coming from the middle of the herd, a puzzling rasping note which was more mechanical than birdlike. As the Saw-whet is a great ventriloquist, it took some time to locate the source of these harsh rasping sounds, but as they persisted, it was possible to center them in a large valley oak that had been left for shade in the corral. The cavity from which the owl worked was about twenty feet up in the main trunk of the great tree, where a limb had rotted away. In the early morning the call was always the same rasping *shee-ahwk*! repeated monotonously. To me it does sound like someone in the final stages of sharpening a cross-cut saw—just putting on the finishing touches. During the night in spring the same owl had a soft regular cooing note which might be transcribed as *quoo-ik*, or *too-too-too*, *kwook*, and which is similar to the call of a Pygmy Owl. If one approaches the nest, this voice will rise in intensity, but the owl makes no other attempt to repel a human intruder.

SAW-WHET ON ALERT

Don Phillips

In the West at least, the local distribution of this owl is often something of a question mark, which makes it a good bird for non-professional watchers who can establish new records. In Colorado it is an infrequent resident, anywhere below 8000 feet, and breeds between 7000 and 8000 feet. To the south, in New Mexico, there are only two breeding records, both in the Sacramento Mountains, while in southern Utah the Saw-whet is a very rare bird of streamside thickets. In Arizona the only breeding record is that of Dr. Mearns on the San Francisco Peaks, dating from the 19th century, but as there are summer observations there, it undoubtedly still breeds in that area. Elsewhere in Arizona it is usually an undetected resident of the mountains of the eastern and central districts, especially the fir clad slopes of the White Mountains, and migrants have been seen in the west of that state.

In the Northeast the Saw-whet Owl likes dense coniferous forests and especially those with marshy areas nearby, but it is also found where there are mixed hardwoods and conifers. Since these little owls have less resistance to extreme weather and the resulting food shortages than big owls do, they tend to drift south with big storms—or sometimes many of these little owls are found dead on the ground after a storm. In some years, such as 1939-1940, there are great southward winter flights in the eastern U. S. (Mumford and Zusi 1958). Another such year was 1965. Among the thousands of little owls which flew south, some 100 specimens were banded in the Middle Atlantic states, with 29 being seen at one spot in Maryland; at least one made it as far as northeastern Florida, where it hunted cotton mice in a wooded swamp dominated by cabbage palms (Lesser & Stickley 1967). Mid-country, the Saw-whet Owl is found from the mountains of Pennsylvania, Ohio, north-central Illinois to southern Nebraska and east-central Missouri. It is a casual winter visitor as far south as Texas.

For some reason Saw-whet Owls in the West are somewhat tardy in nesting, as compared to those of the East. In central New York and in Massachusetts the three to seven eggs are laid in a cavity in April, but on the coast of central California, where climate is no factor at any season, these owls don't nest until the middle of May and in the high Sierras of the state the nesting period falls in June. Other than for that difference of time, the Saw-whet is indifferent as to elevation in the West. In the East, it was assumed for a long time that the Saw-whet, as it lived more southerly, only bred in the high mountains where there was a spruce belt, but in May of 1966 two immature birds were collected in Wayne County, West Virginia, where the altitude is only about 700 feet. All in all, the fact that the Saw-whet is widely distributed, but often very local, and is secretive enough to be seldom seen even when present in fair numbers, suggests that much more can be learned about its distribution and habits. Keep in mind that these owls begin to call as early as February and March, even in the North, and will call through the mating and nesting season. Remember the stick-trick—rap the trunk of any tree with a hole in it—and see which birds appear. Sometimes it will be a Saw-whet Owl and once his residence has been discovered he can be observed and studied at intervals throughout the year, and probably during the following year too.

SAW-WHET PERCHED ON BRANCH OF DOUGLAS FIR TREE   (*Photo by Don & Esther Phillips*)

AFTERWORD

Now that each owl has passed in review we can think of them all once more, retrospectively, as a part of owl history. In the sense used here history is an account of the changing attitudes of men towards owls and of what has been done to them and about them. Perhaps there will also be a note on how the owls themselves have contributed to changing these views. What first appears is that the owls are most often seen in contexts of good and evil, even though we seldom now think of other wild creatures in moral terms. These roles of evil or good are not modern inventions and they had a place long before any state began paying bounties to those who would kill owls. We saw that some American Indians thought of Burrowing Owls as good spirits who protected warriors, or for others the same owl could be one of the "Sickness People," standing for evil and death. Some Indians regarded the Snowy Owl as a Keeper-of-Game diety and thus the most benevolent of good spirits, and the Great Horned Owl was regarded either as a bringer of summer heat and abundant crops, or as an associate of witches, depending upon the place and the season.

As days and nights alternated through unmarked centuries another time came and men with less-balanced views of owls arrived from Europe. Owls to them were like the rest of nature: an opponent to be conquered with arms. Owls were competitors for some of the same small game men wanted and so were seen as enemies to be destroyed. Since owls as a group were symbolic they all suffered together without regard to species. During a winter flight in Ontario alone, a thousand Snowy Owls were shot, just to be stuffed for the mantlepiece, or for nothing at all, and that was just a sign of what was to come to these great white birds when they strayed from their northern homes. More recently I can remember when a seasonal and marshy lake in central California dried up, leaving a perfect feeding ground for untold numbers of meadow mice. Soon a great convocation of Barn Owls gathered round to feed on them, and equally soon the shooters appeared and the "monkey-faced owls" were exploded like clay pigeons in a gallery. Since Barn Owls are as spirits which protect farmers' fields, the owl's good was being repaid with evil.

It was in 1923 when Dawson wrote of the Great Horned Owl in his influential book, *The Birds of California* (II, p. 114):

> "In presenting *Bubo horribilis*, the grizzly bear of the bird world, we shall not be able to offer anything beyond the above named characteristic [it gets an enthusiastic grip on strangers] in his favor. He loves the darkness because his deeds are evil; and after the protecting sun has set, woe betide the mole or rabbit, Partridge, Jay or Chanticleer who dares stir when this monster is a-wing."

This is a surprising statement from a competent ornithologist, but at about the same time there were also more positive views expressed as greater knowledge of owl food habits led to the opinion that at least some owls were on the "good" side. This shift was neither rapid nor complete and since the Great Horned Owl was the most symbolic of owls, it fared the worst. In the year 1961 the Great Horned Owl was protected in 23 states, but unprotected in 27 (Schemnitz 1962); the state of Pennsylvania was still paying a $5.00 bounty for each Horned Owl scalp, a practice which remained in effect until 1965.

By that date, 1965, all scientists and most thoughtful people had accepted the view that predators, including owls, are a necessary part of any working community in nature. Early in this book (pp. 35 - 36) something was said on the kinds of value predators have, including the role a top-predator, like the Great Horned Owl, in keeping a balance of different species in a given community. While these thoughts are not yet common among the public, there has been more willingness to accept predators, including hawks and eagles, as a part of nature rather than as a special class of enemies to be destroyed on sight. Following this trend, Federal protection was extended by law in 1972, to all owls, including the Great Horned Owl. That doesn't mean that the law is fully implemented in every state, but it does for the first time extend the possibility of protection to all of the owls, and local people can encourage enforcement by officials.

Owl history might draw to a conclusion with this account of the road from persecution to protection, but as a matter of fact the story does not end here and there is a second chapter with even more recent events. Curiously enough some owls seem to be in a position to repay us for removing one kind of direct threat to their existence. Their repayment would be in the preservation of certain wilderness environments which are just as important to men as to these owls, thus making the project a kind of joint venture.

Anyone interested in the natural world knows that the greatest threat to all creatures and plants lies in the massive destruction of habitats, which continues today at an accelerating pace. The effects of pesticides and herbicides may not be absolute, but when a habitat is eliminated the whole community of species is gone from that area for some time to come and often forever. Refuges from this desolation are a necessity and while national and state parks, as well as game sanctuaries, provide some relief to beleaguered species there is very little natural space left. In the West the Bureau of Land Management and the U. S. Forest Service—which is to say the American public—already own millions of acres of both harvested forests and untouched areas over which they have control. Much of it is leased for commercial projects and thus subject to mining, grazing and lumbering. While that use is in accord with the public wish, there is also a public desire that a part of these millions of acres should be preserved in their natural state for the protection of all species of wildlife, and with particular attention given to those species which are endangered or rare.

The reader probably already knows that the Southern Bald Eagle, American Peregrine Falcon and the California Condor are birds on the "endangered species" list, but lesser birds such as the Cape Sparrow of Florida are also there. A Federal Register of endangered and threatened wildlife and plants is kept up to date by the Department of the Interior. There are also other categories for animals, birds, plants and other wildlife that may be in particular difficulty. The first owl to receive a special status was the Burrowing Owl which was given a "rare species" designation in the USDI *Red Book* in 1966. "Rare" is a category used when the urgency is less than for species which are "endangered" or "threatened." The Burrowing Owl lost that status in 1968 and in 1973 it was listed by the U. S. Department of the Interior as a "status-undetermined" species; however, one positive result was a study (Zarn 1974b) undertaken by the Bureau of Land Management in their "Habitat Management Series for Unique or Endangered Species." These studies result in small publications giving a description of the species—in this case the Burrowing Owl—its status, population trends, distribution, life history, habitat requirements, protective measures used, and management recommendations. Thus, fundamental information is placed in the hands of Federal officials and the workers who maintain public lands where the species lives, and this pamphlet is also available to anyone interested. While no specific protection is advocated for the Burrowing Owl, further thought is being given to owls living on public domains and that concern may lead to a more reasonable use of rodent pesticides, which were a major factor in the Burrowing Owl's decline.

It remains for another owl, however, to play a possible role in the preservation of certain habitats valuable to all. The Spotted Owl will be remembered as the western counterpart of the Barred Owl, but unlike that species of wide distribution and common occurrence, this species is scattered thinly in the mountains of the West and is uncommon to rare where found. The habitats which may be saved by the Spotted Owl's presence are not just the "wasteland" type of barren ground favored by the Burrowing Owl, but are dense growths of mature timber, usually from 200 to 600 years old and most often with a perennial stream or spring nearby, as these owls like to drink and bathe often. In a way the areas preferred by this owl are perfect parks in themselves, albeit of the wilderness variety since these birds prefer steep and remote canyons. There are few such spots left on private land because timber barons and loggers also like mature forests dominated by trees of saw-timber size, so the remaining owl groves are either in parks or on lands of the U. S. Forest Service and BLM. Timber on National Forest land is regularly sold, in selected blocks, to lumbermen and the latter are not ingrained conservationists. Forsman estimated that of the 123 Spotted Owl sites he studied in Oregon, 49-54% were scheduled for major harvest in the immediate future, so most of those groves will be down by the time this book appears.

It was obvious that before long there would be little or no Spotted Owl habitat left and that soon after that these owls might also vanish. In 1973 the Spotted Owl was listed in the USDI *Red Book* of threatened species (later changed). That status encouraged a number of study projects which made thorough surveys of this owl's biology and habits, and made suggestions as to how it could best be protected. One of these studies came from the BLM in Denver (Zarn 1974a), while others were undertaken in the forests of California by a cooperative effort of the U. S. Forest Service and the California Department of Fish and Game (Gould 1974). In Oregon, studies are being done by the Co-operative Wildlife Research Unit of Oregon State University at Corvallis, one result being Forsman's study of 1976, with other research carried out by the BLM out of Medford, Oregon.

According to Robert Maben, Staff Biologist for the Oregon State Dept. of Fish and Wildlife, the Spotted Owl has been officially listed as a "threatened species" in Oregon since March of 1975. The USDI dropped the Spotted Owl from its threatened and endangered list and its Federal status is now that of a "unique" species. In California that makes it a companion of the Prairie Falcon and the tule elk which are also listed as unique. A "unique" species is one kept in limbo for the time, as it is not thought to be in any immediate danger of extinction, but it is a species which needs more study to determine how best to encourage the maintenance or increase of species numbers, and also needs some special protection while the facts are being gathered. By an intensive two-year study in California 263 Spotted Owls were sighted, representing 192 locations—not a crowded condition certainly, but somewhat more than expected.

Suggestions for protecting this owl have come from biologists in both Oregon and California. Forsman noted that present Oregon timber practices call for short rotations in forest harvest with trees on private land falling to the chain saw every 56 to 77 years while those on federal lands are cut at 75 to 80 year intervals, meaning that when old groves disappear they are never replaced. He proposes that some old owl groves on public lands be made into multiple use preserves and held for 300 year rotations. In California, Gould has suggested a no-cut area around known Spotted Owl nests of 660 feet, with three times that diameter protected during the foraging stage of young owls, although this outer area might be subject to cutting at later dates (Gould 1974 and personal communication 1977). Both biologists urge that related perennial streams and springs be included in the protected area around nesting sites. Since Spotted Owls are sedentary, they will live and nest in the same spot year after year, making the protection of specific groves feasible. Wildlife biologist Larry A. Forbis of the U. S. Forest Service writes that presently there are no protected owl sites in the Klamath National Forest, but that 17 such sites are known there and there are no immediate conflicts between timber sales and Spotted Owl groves. There are proposals for protective areas of either 80 acres or 300 acres around each nest site in the Klamath.

Where the matter stands now was expressed by Harry J. Taylor who is Recreation, Range and Wildlife Officer for the U. S. Forest Service. In a letter to rangers and staff (Nov. 1976) he notes that this owl has no current status as either threatened or endangered, and states: ". . . Therefore, the spotted owl will not enjoy protection under the Endangered Species act of 1973. The Forest Service is not legally obligated to provide habitat for spotted owls." Then, after reviewing diminishing numbers, he mentions "cold hard facts" and "cost in terms of ultimate timber production," reminding one of the great gap between the biologist's realization of what should be done and a government agency's ability to implement that knowledge. He urges that protection for this owl be combined with other constraints on streamside zones where many of the Spotted Owls live, thus saving a portion of the groves.

How you and I would benefit from the preservation of the remaining Spotted Owl groves is clear enough, but why the owls need them deserves comment. Other species of owls, such as the Screech Owl, which can live in any kind of environment so long as there are tree hollows for nesting, adapt very well to changes brought about by man and can thus persist. In the eastern states the Great Horned Owl will get along if only a few woodlots are left among the plowed fields, even though they may prefer deeper forests. The Spotted Owl, on the other hand, needs a very special kind of forest for its home. There must be a mature, large tree forest of dense growth, with a crown closure of at least 80%, and an understory for the young owls to use as perches while they learn to fly, and it should have permanent water nearby.

These owls never object to the presence of humans, as they are completely unafraid and able to live and breed in national parks which have tens or hundreds of thousands of visitors each year. A Spotted Owl nest is likely to be a hundred feet above the ground and in a

secluded nook where they are active only at night, so there is no con-
flict with people. Even though these owls are few in number and widely
scattered, they are not hermits and a single preserved grove will not
suffice. These owls, like other birds, need replacement individuals for
pair formation so they rarely occur as isolated pairs and there is usually
no more than five or six miles between them (Gould 1974). A few
places are favored with concentrations of these owls, as in one section
of Trinity County, California where a drainage thirty miles long and six
miles wide provides home groves for sixteen pairs which are spread
along at about one and a half to two mile intervals. Thus if Spotted
Owls are to be maintained, clusters of owl groves will have to be preserved, as they are in state and national parks.

Preservation of the remaining Spotted Owl groves on National
Forest or other public lands is still an uncertain matter and the pressures
against sparing pockets of old forests are great, despite the invaluable
rewards to ourselves and future generations. If the preserved owl groves
include the nearby streams and watershed, the area could be used simul-
taneously for a study-research plot where the next generation of biologists could learn their trade by studying a complete old-growth plant
and wildlife community, and as a museum or park for the use of people
who would like to see how things were in untouched woods. There are
not so many of these groves (mere crumbs to a timber merchant) that it
would be inconvenient to save them—after all, 300 acres for each of the
17 groves in the vast Klamath National Forest totals only a little over
5000 acres, and the public already owns them. One of the recommendations of the Oregon Department of Fish and Wildlife is for placing the
Spotted Owl on the national list of threatened fish and wildlife. Since
the Act of 1973 states that a "threatened species" is one that may become endangered in *all, or a significant portion, of its range,* this owl
qualifies through its tenuous foothold in the forests of Oregon. If
placed on the national list of threatened species, Federal agencies such
as the Forest Service and the Bureau of Land Management would be
legally obligated to give the Spotted Owl some protection. Since public
feelings, if known, will inevitably have weight in the decisions made,
one should express his opinion.*

* To elected representatives, to officials in the Department of Interior, and,
specifically, to: The Bureau of Land Management, U. S. Department of the
Interior, Washington, D. C. 20240.

It may yet come about that a little known species of owl will be the means of saving not only its own kind, but also the parklike owl groves for future generations of owls and humans to enjoy together. If so, it will be a very wise move in owl history.

ALTERNATIVE COMMON NAMES FOR OWLS

The common names for all of our birds, including owls, have been standardized since the 5th edition of *The A. O. U. Check-list of North American Birds* (1957) and its supplements. These English names used for the owls in the text of this book are now the only official common names. At the same time the American Ornithologist's Union eliminated common names for each different subspecies, leaving but the single name for the species and its components. New shoes may be uncomfortable at first, but the simplification and standardization of the plethora of common names should have everyone's support.

However, both the older names and the subspecies names remain in many books that one may consult, and often a reader may know only an alternative name—for example "monkey-faced" owl for the Barn Owl, or one may have grown up saying Richardson's owl and have to think twice to remember that it is now a Boreal Owl. For these reasons this list is presented as a convenience, for connecting alternative names to the official common names. The latter are given first and are, appropriately, capitalized.

1. Barn Owl

    American barn owl
    golden owl
    monkey-faced owl

2. Screech Owl

    common screech owl
    little owl
    shivering owl

    Subspecies names:

Aiken's screech owl	Mexican screech owl
Brewster's screech owl	Nebraska screech owl
California screech owl	Pasadena screech owl
eastern screech owl	Rocky Mountain screech owl
Florida screech owl	saguaro screech owl
Guadalupe screech owl	southern screech owl
Hasbrouck's screech owl	So. Calif. screech owl

Kennicott's screech owl   Texas screech owl
MacFarlane's screech owl   Yuma screech owl

3.   Whiskered Owl

spotted screech owl
Arizona whiskered owl

4.   Flammulated Owl

flammulated screech owl
scops owl (also used for others)

5.   Great Horned Owl

horned owl
hoot owl

Subspecies names:

Arctic great horned owl   northwestern great horned owl
dusky great horned owl   Pacific great horned owl
dwarf great horned owl   St. Michael great horned owl
Labrador great horned owl   tundra great horned owl
Montana great horned owl   western great horned owl

6.   Snowy Owl

American snowy owl
Arctic owl
great white owl
white owl

7.   Hawk Owl

American hawk owl
day owl
Hudsonian owl

8.   Pygmy Owl

mountain pygmy owl

Subspecies names:

California pygmy owl   northern pygmy owl
coast pygmy owi   Rocky Mountain pygmy owl
Hoskin's pygmy owl   Vancouver pygmy owl

9.   Ferruginous Owl

   ferruginous pygmy owl
   streaked pygmy owl

Subspecies name:

   cactus pygmy owl

10.   Elf Owl

Subspecies names:

   Sanford's elf owl
   Texas elf owl
   Whitney's elf owl

11.   Burrowing Owl

   billy owl
   ground owl
   howdy owl
   prairie dog owl

Subspecies names:

   Florida burrowing owl
   western burrowing owl

12.   Barred Owl

   swamp owl
   wood owl

Subspecies names:

   northern barred owl
   Florida barred owl
   Texas barred owl

13.   Spotted Owl

   western barred owl
   wood owl

Subspecies names:

   Arizona (or Mexican) spotted owl
   California spotted owl
   northern spotted owl

14.   Great Gray Owl

      spectral owl

15.   Long-eared Owl

      American long-eared owl
      cat owl

    Subspecies name:

      western long-eared owl

16.   Short-eared Owl

      grass owl
      marsh owl
      prairie owl

    Subspecies name:

      northern short-eared owl

17.   Boreal Owl

      Arctic saw-whet owl
      Richardson's owl
      Tengmalm's owl

18.   Saw-whet Owl

    Subspecies names:

      Acadian owl
      Queen Charlotte owl

THE SCIENTIFIC NAMES OF THESE OWLS
AND THEIR MEANINGS

The scientific name of any creature consists of two Latin words, the first of which is capitalized and represents the genus, while the second word of the name is without a beginning capital letter, and it represents the species. These names are usually in italic type face to make them stand out from the surrounding text. Most everyone knows that a scientific name makes some kind of sense, but it is hard to say just what the sense is, even if one knows a little Latin. To begin with, the scholar who first named the bird had a chance to make that name descriptive—but only by way of a single word. This extreme shorthand is further limited by the fact that seldom does the same person get to name both the genus and the species, so the two parts of the name often do not add up to greater meanings. Furthermore, the names of genera have been shifted around a number of times in the last hundred years. For example, the Barn Owl belonged to the genus *Aluco* at the end of the 19th century, while it now belongs to the genus *Tyto*.

These qualifications are to warn the reader not to expect any great revelations from the translation into English of the scientific names of our owls. Nevertheless, the Latin names do have meanings and one interested in owls may wish to know what these are. Many of the names come from ancient Greek owl names. It naturally occurred to the scientist in naming our own owls that he should use these earlier names, but after the best known Greek names were used still others were needed, and therefore obscure names were also borrowed. A case in point is the first genus on our list.

1.   Barn Owl. *Tyto alba.*

Tyto was a Greek name for a "night owl" and likely for one with a "hoot," since both *tyto* and its Latin form, *tutu*, indicate the "toot toot" call of an owl. The Barn Owl was found in Greece, as well as in many other parts of the world, but it notably does not "hoot," so whatever the Greek night-owl was, it was not a Barn Owl. The species name, *alba*, is more descriptive as it means "white" and the Barn Owl is distinctly white on the underside when seen in dim light.

2.   Screech Owl. *Otus asio.*

"Otos" was a Greek owl with ear tufts. The Screech Owl has such tufts and the Greeks had a related bird in the Scops Owl, but the name probably referred to an owl further down on our list (No. 15). The specific name, *asio*, was a Roman name for a "Horned" Owl, and a word apparently derived from the Hebrew.

3.   Whiskered Owl. *Otus trichopsis.*

The genus name is the same as above, while the specific name is a compound of Greek words which add up to: "hairy-countenance." Thus a perfect fit which agrees with the common name.

4.   Flammulated Owl. *Otus flammeolus.*

Here is the same genus again. The specific name is a diminutive of the Latin word for "flaming." The Flammulated Owl is very tiny, weighing only an ounce or two, so the diminutive is apt—"little red owl."

5.   Great Horned Owl. *Bubo virginianus.*

The genus name, *Bubo*, was the Latin name for the Eagle Owl and the word apparently comes from a verb meaning "to hoot" on a low pitch." The Eagle Owl belongs to the same genus as our Great Horned Owl, so the name fits exactly. There are several lines of classical poetry which make use of this name, as in Ovid:

ignavus bubo, dirum mortalibus omen.

Which might be freely translated as: "listless Bubo, bird of omen evil to mortals." *Metamorphoses V, 550.* Or to wrench a segment from Virgil:

visa viri, nox cum terras obscura teneret;
solaque culminibus ferali carmine bubo. . .

Even more freely translated, the lines call up the night's shadowing the earth and this owl's song, *carmine bubo*, which bodes ill.

The specific name of the Great Horned Owl, *virginianus*, means "of Virginia," from whence our species was described in 1788.

6.   Snowy Owl. *Nyctea scandiaca.*

The name of the genus derives from an adjective meaning "nocturnal." It is from the Greek. The specific name, *scandiaca*, relates the bird to Scandinavia. The species is found in northern regions around the entire world, but was first named by the Swedish naturalist Linnaeus, who then called it *Nyctea nyctea*; the present specific name was applied later.

7.   Hawk Owl. *Surnia ulula.*

The species, in this case, was described by Linnaeus long before the genus name was created. *Surnia* as a genus name originated with Duméril in 1806 and, since there is no known etymology for the word, it is considered an "arbitrary" name. There is some possibility that the name was based on a modern Greek word for a Screech Owl. The specific name *ulula* is a genuine Latin word which, like *tutu*, imitates the owl's hoots, and the name was applied by Pliny to the Screech Owl. Behind the Latin was the Greek word, *ololuxo*, "I howl," "I shriek" or "I wail," a set of possibilities which would include numerous kinds of owls and their calls.

8.   Pygmy Owl. *Glaucidium gnoma.*

The name *glaux* was used by the ancient Greeks for the Little Owl of Europe (*Athene noctua*). That was the owl sacred to Athena, and hence connected with wisdom. The word-form *glaucidium* is a diminuitive of *glaux*, and thus an apt name for an owl even smaller than the Little Owl. The specific name, *gnoma*, relates back to a Greek word with the same spelling meaning "decision" or "opinion," such as might be handed down by a wise judge. A Latin word related to *gnoma* refers to the small spirits who lived in caves, which gives us the English word "gnome." These are the "knowing ones" of folklore, who are small as well as wise.

9.   Ferruginous Owl. *Glaucidium brasilianum.*

The genus here is the same as for the previous species. There is a novelty in the species name in that our present common name, Ferruginous—meaning "rusty"—was once the scientific name (*ferrugineum*). As time passed it was discovered that this species of the southwestern U. S.

and Mexico was identical with one described previously from Brazil. Therefore it had been given the name *brasilianum*, and that name being the older had priority over the "rusty" designation.

10.   Elf Owl. *Micrathene whitneyi.*

When the European Little Owl was mentioned on the preceding page, its genus name was given as *Athene*. That name properly related it to the goddess to whom the owl was sacred. The newly discovered American owl was smaller, so Dr. Coues constructed the genus from a compound: *mikros*, Greek for "small" and *Athene*. When Dr. Cooper, the famous western ornithologist, named the species in 1861, in a publication of the California Academy of Sciences, he named it *whitneyi* in honor of J. D. Whitney who was Director of the Geological Survey of California.

11.   Burrowing Owl. *Athene [Speotyto] cunicularia.*

The former genus name, *Speotyto*, is again a compound of two words: *speos*, a Greek word for "cave" or "excavation," and *tyto*. The latter meaning "owl," as seen in the genus name under (1) above. The genus *Athene* is named after the goddess Athene, daughter of Zeus; among her other attributes she was goddess of the clear sky and pure air. She was protectress of the city of Athens. The Little Owl, *Athene noctua*, was sacred to her and our Burrowing Owl is now placed in the same genus. The Latin word *cunicularius* means "miner," so the full name may be a little redundant, but it certainly stands for a Burrowing Owl.

12.   Barred Owl. *Strix varia.*

The word *strix* was used in both Greek and Latin for a "screech owl." It means a shrill or strident sound of any kind, and both "strident" and "stridulous" are English derivatives. The owl called *Strix* appears in the Greek myths recorded by Antoninus Liberalis, *Metamorphoses*, Book XXI, 4,5., in which Polyphontes encounters an owl of this name whose voice presages war and sedition. Ovid gives a horrendous description of these owls: "goggle their eyes, their beaks are formed for rapine, their wings are blotched with gray, their claws fitted with hooks. They fly by night and attack nurseless children, and defile their bodies, snatched from their cradles. They are said to rend the flesh of sucklings with their beaks, and their throats are full of the blood which they have drunk." This section of the Latin poem by Ovid ends with *"est illis strigibus nomen,"* "strix is their name." Ovid, *Fasti,* vi. 130-140. It will be noted that in this Latin form the name is also the source for the family name of the typical owls: **Strigidae.**

Ovid goes on to note that a supernatural, rather than a mere bird was involved and in his story a crane exchanges animal entrails as surrogates for those of the babe, and establishes the Roman custom of sacrificing by entrail offerings.

After these complications related to the generic name, one may be happy to know that the specific name of the Barred Owl, *varia,* merely means "different." Presumably the difference would be from an European owl of the genus which was described earlier. Unfortunately, the genus name *Strix* was first used for other owls (both for the Snowy and the Great Horned) so this owl is not indicated as different from its present relatives in the genus *Strix.*

13. Spotted Owl. *Strix occidentalis.*

The Spotted Owl has the same genus as the previous owl. The specific name, *occidentalis,* means "western," and correctly locates the owl in the western part of the U. S.

14. Great Gray Owl. *Strix nebulosa.*

Again, it has the same genus name. The Latin word *nebulosus* means, "misty, foggy, cloudy, dark." The word describes the spectral presence of this owl, which inhabits the far north of Europe and Asia as well as North America.

15. Long-eared Owl. *Asio otus.*

Here we come to a kind of scientific joke. It will be noted that the name of this owl is the exact opposite of the Screech Owl (2), with the genus name of that bird becoming the specific name of this owl, and the specific name of the Screech Owl becoming the generic name here. That is very confusing, but part of the blame can be laid to a necessary shifting of scientific names. *Asio* here is again the Roman name for a horned or eared owl, which fits the Long-eared, or the Screech

Owl. The specific name *otus* does join much better here, because the Greek name *otos* likely referred to either this bird or the following species (see Aristotle, *Historia Animalium*, viii, 12., where he describes the "eared owl"). Since the Greek owl in question was migratory, inhabited open country, and was diurnal, it describes the next species, the Short-eared Owl, better than this one (see: D'Arcy W. Thompson, *A Glossary of Greek Birds*, Oxford 1895, p. 201).

16.   Short-eared Owl. *Asio flammeus*.

The Short-eared Owl carries the same genus name as the previous species. Once again *flammeus* is the word "flaming," and actually an overstatement for the tawny-brown color of this owl.

17.   Boreal Owl. *Aegolius funereus*.

Aegolius was another Greek owl name and probably referred to the Tawny Owl (*Strix aluco*) of Europe, although there is some dispute on that. *Funereus* of course means funeral; the owl's call sounding a mourning bell for the dead.

18.   Saw-whet Owl. *Aegolius acadicus*.

The Saw-whet has the same genus name as the Boreal Owl. The specific name of this owl refers to Acadia, the region in the Northeast U. S. and adjoining Canada which was the setting for Longfellow's poem "Evangaline." This owl was named in 1788, from that part of our country.

REFERENCES AND FURTHER READING

The best next step for one who wishes to know more about these owls is to consult the detailed state bird books, such as E. H. Forbush's *The Birds of Massachusetts and Other New England States*, 1925-29, or W. L. Dawson's *The Birds of California*, 1923. There are similar books for most states, containing detailed information often not available in shorter and more recent handbooks. The state books are not all listed here, but are easily located in any public library, for the particular states or areas from which the reader observes.

A second step is to learn more about those species of owls which the reader has discovered in his area, and the aim of the selected list which follows is to guide him into the extensive literature on our owls. Many of these articles are illustrated, and most are short and easy to read, once located. For that purpose one will have to consult college libraries, or find a bird enthusiast who subscribes to some of the basic ornithological journals in which these articles have been published.

Altman, S. A. 1956. "Avian Mobbing Behavior and Predator Recognition." *Condor* 58:241-249.

American Ornithologists' Union. 1957. *The A. O. U. Check-list of North American Birds.* 5th edition. Baltimore, Md.

———1976. "Thirty-third Supplement to A. O. U. Check-list." *Auk* 93:875-879.

Ames, P. L. 1967. "Overlapping Nesting by a Pair of Barn Owls." *Wilson Bull.* 79:451-452.

Armstrong, W. H. 1958. "Nesting and Food Habits of the Long-eared Owl in Michigan." Pub. Mich. State Univ. Biol. Series 1:63-96.

Bailey, F. M. 1928. *Birds of New Mexico.* N. M. Dept. of Game & Fish, and Bureau of Biological Survey, Washington, D. C.

Baldwin, P. H. & J. R. Koplin. 1966. "The Boreal Owl as a Pleistocene Relict in Colorado." *Condor* 8:299-300.

Banfield, A. W. F. 1947. "A Study of Winter Feeding Habits of the Short-eared Owl (*Asio flammeus*) in the Toronto Region." Can. J. Res. 25D:45-65.

Baumgartner, F. M. 1939. "Territory and Population in the Great Horned Owl." *Auk* 56:274-282.

Behle, W. H., J. B. Bushman & C. M. Greenhalgh. 1958. *Birds of the Kanab Area and Adjacent High Plateaus of Southern Utah.* U. of Utah Biol. Series, XI, No. 7. Salt Lake City, Utah.

Bendire, Capt. C. 1892. *Life Histories of North American Birds, with special reference to their breeding habits and eggs.* U. S. Nat. Mus., Special Bull. No. 1, pp. 325-414 and Pl. XII.

Bent, A. C. 1961. *Life Histories of North American Birds of Prey,* Part Two: Hawks, Falcons, Caracaras and Owls. N. Y., Dover.

Bergtold, W. H. 1928. *A Guide to Colorado Birds.* Denver, Colo.

Billeb, S. L. 1962. "Occurrence of Great Gray Owls in Mono County, California." *Condor* 64:164-165.

Bond, R. M. 1939. "Observations on Raptorial Birds in the Lava Beds— Tule Lake Region of Northern California." *Condor* 41:54-6l.

Brock, E. M. 1958. "Some Prey of the Pygmy Owl." *Condor* 60:338.

Burton, J. A. (ed.) 1973. *Owls of the World.* E. P. Dutton, New York.

Cameron, A. & P. Parnall. 1971. *The Nightwatchers.* Four Winds Press, N. Y.

Campbell, J. M. 1969. "Owls of the Central Brooks Range, Alaska." *Auk* 86:565-568.

Clark, R. J. 1975. *A Field Study of the Short-Eared Owl, Asio flammeus* (Pontoppidan) *in North America.* Wildlife Monographs No. 47. Louisville, Kent.

Coulombe, H. N. 1971. "Behavior and Population Ecology of the Burrowing Owl, *Speotyto cunicularia,* in the Imperial Valley of California." *Condor,* Vol. 73:162-176.

Craighead, J. J. & F. C. Craighead. 1969. *Hawks, Owls and Wildlife.* N. Y., Dover.

Dawson, W. H. 1923. *The Birds of California.* Vol. III. South Moulton Co., San Diego, Calif.

Dice, L. R. 1945. "Minimum Intensities of Illumination Under Which Owls Can Find Dead Prey By Sight." *American Naturalist* 79: 385-416.

Dickey, D. R. 1914. "The Nesting of the Spotted Owl." *Condor* 16: 193-202.

Dixon, J. S. 1944. "A Great Gray Owl Observed in Yosemite National Park." *Condor* 46:244.

Dubois, A. D. 1924. "The Nuptial Song-flight of the Short-eared Owl." *Auk* 41:260-263.

Earhart, C. M. & N. K. Johnson. 1970. "Size, Dimorphism and Food Habits of North American Owls." *Condor* 72:251-264.

Eaton, W. F. 1924. "Richardson's Owl in Vermont in Summer." *Auk* 41:155-156.

Errington, P. L. 1930. "The Pellet Analysis Method of Raptor Food Habits Study." *Condor* 32:292-296.

———1932. "Food Habits of Southern Wisconsin Raptors," Pt. 1. Owls. *Condor* 34:176-186.

———& F. Hammerstrom & F. M. Hammerstrom. 1940. *The Great Horned Owl and its Prey in North-Central U. S.* Iowa State Col. of Agr., Agric. Res. Bull. 277:759-850.

Evans, F. C. & J. T. Emlen Jr. 1947. "Ecological Notes on the Prey Selected by a Barn Owl." *Condor* 49:3-9.

Fitch, H. S. 1947. "Predation by Owls in the Sierran Foothills of California." *Condor* 49:137-151.

Flemming, J. H. 1916. "The Saw-whet Owl of the Queen Charlotte Islands." *Auk* 33:420-423.

Forbush, E. H. 1927. *Birds of Massachusetts and Other New England States.* Vol. II. Mass. Dept. of Agric., Norwood, Mass.

Forsman, Eric. 1976. "A Preliminary Investigation of the Spotted Owl in Oregon." MS thesis, Ore. State U., Corvallis, Ore. pp. 5 + 127.

Gabrielson, I. N. & S. G. Jewett. 1940. *Birds of Oregon.* Oregon State U., Corvalis, Oregon. (Reprinted as *Birds of the Pacific Northwest.* 1970. Dover Pubs., New York, N. Y.)

Goodrich, A. L. 1946. *Birds in Kansas.* Kansas State Board of Agric., Topeka, Kansas.

Gould, G. I., Jr. 1974. "The Status of the Spotted Owl in California." Calif. Dept. of Fish and Game, The Resources Agency, Sacramento, California. pp. 36 & 19.

Graber, R. R. 1962. "Food and Oxygen Consumption in Three Species of Owls (Strigidae)." *Condor* 64:473-487.

Granfield, W. M. 1937. "Nesting of the Saw-whet Owl." *Condor* 39:185-187.

Grant, R. A. 1965. "The Burrowing Owl in Minnesota." *Loon* 37:2-17.

Grinnell, J. 1914. *An Account of the Mammals and Birds of the Lower Colorado Valley.* Univ. of Calif. Pubs. in Zool. 12, No. 4, Berkeley, Calif.

———& A. H. Miller. 1944. *The Distribution of the Birds of California.* Pacific Coast Avifauna, No. 27., Berkeley, Calif.

Gross, A. O. 1947. "Cyclic Invasions of the Snowy Owl and the Migrations of 1945-1946." *Auk* 64:584-601.

Grossman, M. L. and J. Hamlet. 1964. *Birds of Prey of the World*. Clarkson N. Potter, New York.

Hagar, D. C. Jr. 1957. "Nesting Populations of Red-tailed Hawks and Horned Owls in Central New York State." *Wilson Bull.* 69:263-272.

Hanson, W. C. 1971. "Snowy Owl Incursions in South-eastern Washington and the Pacific Northwest (1966-67)." *Condor* 73:114-116.

Henderson, A. D. 1919. "Nesting of the American Hawk Owl." *Oologist* 36:59-63.

Howard, W. E. 1958. "Food and Pellet Formation of a Horned Owl." *Auk* 70:145-150.

Howell, T. R. 1964. "Notes on Incubation and Nestling Temperatures and Behavior of Captive Owls." *Wilson Bull.* 76:28-36.

Jacot, E. C. 1931. "Notes on the Spotted and Flammulated Screech Owls in Arizona." *Condor* 33:8-11.

Jewett, S. G. *et al.* 1953. *Birds of Washington State*. U. of Wash. Press, Seattle, Wash.

Johnson, N. K. 1954. "Food of the Long-eared Owl in Southern Washoe County Nevada." *Condor* 56:52.

———& W. C. Russell. 1962. "Distributional Data on Certain Owls in the Western Great Basin." *Condor* 64:513-514. (Has weights on flammulated owls.)

Kelso, L. H. 1940. "Variation of the External Ear Opening in the Strigidae." *Wilson Bull.* 52:24-29.

Lesser, F. H. & A. R. Stickley. 1967. "Occurrence of the Saw-whet Owl in Florida." *Auk* 84:425.

Ligon, J. David. 1963. "Breeding Range Expansion of the Burrowing Owl in Florida." *Auk* 80:167-168.

———1968. *The Biology of the Elf Owl, Micrathene whitneyi*. Univ. of Michigan, Museum of Zool., Misc. Pub. No. 136, Ann Arbor, Mich.

———1969. "Some Aspects of Temperature Relations in Small Owls." *Auk* 86:458-472.

Ligon, J. Stokley. 1926. "Habits of the Spotted Owl." *Auk* 43:421-429.

———1961. *New Mexico Birds and Where to Find Them*. U. of New Mexico Press, Albuquerque, N. M.

Linsdale, J. M. 1936. *The Birds of Nevada*. Pacific Coast Avifauna No. 23, Berkeley, Calif.

Marshall, Joe T., Jr. 1939. "Territorial Behavior of the Flammulated Screech Owl." *Condor* 41:71-78.

———1942. "Food and Habitat of the Spotted Owl." *Condor* 44:66-67.

———1957. *Birds of Pine-Oak Woodland in Southern Arizona and Adjacent Mexico.* Pacific Coast Avifauna No. 32. Berkeley, Calif.

———1967. *Parallel Variation in North and Middle American Screech Owls.* Monographs of the Western Foundation of Vertebrate Zoology, No. 1:1-72.

———1974. "Strigiformes." Article in *The New Encyclopedia Britannica* (Macropaedia, vol. 17). Encyclopedia Britannica, Inc., Chicago, Ill.

Marti, C. D. 1974. "Feeding Ecology of Four Sympatric Owls." *Condor* 76:45-61.

———1976. "A Review of Prey Selection by the Long-eared Owl." *Condor* 78:331-336.

Martin, D. J. 1973. "Selected Aspects of Burrowing Owl Ecology and Behavior." *Condor* 75:446-456.

Maser, C., E. W. Hammer and S. H. Anderson. 1971. "Food Habits of the Burrowing Owl in Central Oregon." *Northwest Science* 45:19-26.

Mayr, E. and M. Mayr. 1954. "Tail Molt of Small Owls." *Auk* 71:172-178.

Miller, A. H. 1934. "The Vocal Apparatus of Some North American Owls." *Condor* 36:204-213.

———& L. Miller. 1951. "Geographic Variation of the Screech Owls of the Deserts of Western North America." *Condor* 53:171-177.

Miller, L. 1952. "Auditory Recognition of Predators." *Condor* 54:89-92.

Mumford, R. E. & R. L. Zusi. 1958. "Note on Movements, Territory, and Habitat of Wintering Saw-whet Owls." *Auk* 70:188-191.

Murie, O. J. 1929. "Nesting of the Snowy Owl." *Condor* 31:3-12.

Nero, R. W. 1969. "The Status of the Great Gray Owl in Manitoba, with Special Reference to the 1968-69 Influx." *Blue Jay* 27:191-209.

———1977. "Great Gray Owl Nests." *Manitoba Nature* 17:4-11.

Orians, G. & F. Kuhlman. 1956. "Red-tailed Hawk and Horned Owl Populations in Wisconsin." *Condor* 58:371-385.

Payne, R. S. 1962. "How the Barn Owl Locates Prey by Hearing." *Living Bird* 1:151-159.

Peterson, R. T. 1947. *A Field Guide to the Birds.* Houghton Mifflin Co., Boston, Mass.

—— 1961. *A Field Guide to Western Birds.* Houghton Mifflin Co., Boston, Mass.

—— 1963. *A Field Guide to the Birds of Texas.* Houghton Mifflin Co., Boston, Mass.

Phillips, A., J. Marshall, & G. Monson. 1964. *The Birds of Arizona.* The U. of Arizona Press, Tucson, Ariz.

Randle, W. & R. Austing. 1952. "Ecological Notes on Long-eared and Saw-whet Owls in Southwestern Ohio." *Ecology* 33:422-426.

Robbins, C. S., B. Bruun, & H. S. Zim. 1966. *A Guide to Field Identification, Birds of North America.* Golden Press, N. Y.

Roberts, T. S. 1936. *The Birds of Minnesota,* Vol. I. U. of Minnesota Press, Minneapolis, Minn.

Ross, A. 1969. *Ecological Aspects of the Food Habits of Insectivorous Screech Owls.* Proc. Western Foundation of Vertebrate Zool. 1: 301-344.

Santee, R. & W. Granfield. 1939. "Behavior of the Saw-whet Owl on Its Nesting Grounds." *Condor* 41:3-9.

Saunders, A. A. 1921. *A Distributional List of the Birds of Montana.* Pacific Coast Avifauna, No. 14. Berkeley, Calif.

Schemnitz, S. D. 1962. "Notes on the Food Habits of the Great Horned Owl in Oklahoma." *Condor* 64:328-329.

Sumner, E. L., Jr. 1928. "Notes on the Development of Young Screech Owls." *Condor* 30:333-338.

Sutton, G. M. 1967. *Oklahoma Birds.* U. of Oklahoma Press, Norman, Oklahoma.

—— & D. F. Parmelee. 1956. "Breeding of the Snowy Owl in Southeastern Baffin Island." *Condor* 58:273-282.

Swarth, H. S. 1904. *Birds of the Huachuca Mountains,* Arizona. Pacific Coast Avifauna, No. 4. Los Angeles, Calif.

Taverner, P. A. 1934. *The Birds of Canada.* Nat. Mus. of Canada, Bull. No. 72. Ottawa, Ont.

Taylor, A. L. Jr. & E. Forsman. 1976. "Recent Range Extensions of the Barred Owl in Western North America, Including the First Records for Oregon." *Condor* 78:560-561.

Terrill, L. M. 1931. "Nesting of the Saw-whet Owl in the Montreal District." *Auk* 48:169-174.

Thomsen, L. 1971. "Behavior and Ecology of Burrowing Owls on the Oakland Municipal Airport." *Condor* 73:177-192.

Todd, W. E. Clyde. 1963. *Birds of the Labrador Peninsula and Adjacent Areas.* University of Toronto Press, Toronto.

Tyler, John G. 1913. *Some Birds of the Fresno District, Calif.* Pacific Coast Avifauna No. 9., Hollywood, Calif.

Walker, L. W. 1943. "Nocturnal Observations on Elf Owls." *Condor* 45:165-167.

Wallace, G. J. 1948. *The Barn Owl in Michigan.* Mich. State Coll. of Agr. Exp. Stat., Bull. 208. East Lansing, Mich.

Watson, A. 1957. "The Behavior, Breeding and Food Ecology of the Snowy Owl, *Nyctea scandiaca.*" *Ibis* 99:419-462.

Winter, Jon. 1971. "Some Critical Notes on Finding and Seeing the Flammulated Owl. *Birding* 3:205-209.

———1974. "The Distribution of the Flammulated Owl in California." *Western Birds* 5:25-44.

"The Winter Season, Dec. 1, 1976 - Feb. 28, 1977." 1977. In *American Birds* 3(3):304-377. New York, N. Y.

Zarn, Mark. 1974a. "Spotted Owl, *Strix occidentalis.*" Habitat Management Series for Unique or Endangered Species, Report No. 10. Bureau of Land Management, Denver Federal Center, Denver, Colo.

———1974b. "Burrowing Owl, *speotyto cunicularia hypugaea.*" Ibid. Report No. 11.

INDEX